CRITICAL THINKING SKILLS

How to Understand and Use Critical Thinking Skills

(A Practical Step by Step Guide to Developing Critical Thinking Skills)

Rossana Crabtree

Published by Tomas Edwards

© **Rossana Crabtree**

All Rights Reserved

Critical Thinking Skills: How to Understand and Use Critical Thinking Skills (A Practical Step by Step Guide to Developing Critical Thinking Skills)

ISBN 978-1-990373-29-9

All rights reserved. No part of this guide may be reproduced in any form without permission in writing from the publisher except in the case of brief quotations embodied in critical articles or reviews.

Legal & Disclaimer

The information contained in this book is not designed to replace or take the place of any form of medicine or professional medical advice. The information in this book has been provided for educational and entertainment purposes only.

The information contained in this book has been compiled from sources deemed reliable, and it is accurate to the best of the Author's knowledge; however, the Author cannot guarantee its accuracy and validity and cannot be held liable for any errors or omissions. Changes are periodically made to this book. You must consult your doctor or get professional medical advice before using any of the suggested remedies, techniques, or information in this book.

Upon using the information contained in this book, you agree to hold harmless the Author from and against any damages, costs, and expenses, including any legal fees potentially resulting from the application of any of the information provided by this guide. This disclaimer applies to any damages or injury caused by the use and application, whether directly or indirectly, of any advice or information presented, whether for breach of contract, tort, negligence, personal injury, criminal intent, or under any other cause of action.

You agree to accept all risks of using the information presented inside this book. You need to consult a professional medical practitioner in order to ensure you are both able and healthy enough to participate in this program.

Table of Contents

INTRODUCTION 1

CHAPTER 1: START THINKING 4

CHAPTER 2: THE BENEFITS OF CRITICAL THINKING FOR YOU 13

CHAPTER 3: PROBLEM SOLVING STRATEGIES 16

CHAPTER 4: BIAS, STEREOTYPES, AND PREJUDICE 44

CHAPTER 5: GUIDANCE ON SOUND REASONING AND TEXTUAL ANALYSIS 56

CHAPTER 6: MAKING MENTAL MODELS WORK FOR YOU 78

CHAPTER 7: HOW TO LEARN THE BASICS OF PSYCHOLOGY 92

CHAPTER 8: THE MINDSET 105

CHAPTER 9: MAKING DECISIONS UNDER PRESSURE 120

CHAPTER 10: DEAL WITH A PROBLEM 135

CHAPTER 11: THE ART OF PATTERN RECOGNITION AND CHUNKING 142

CHAPTER 12: CONNECTING CRITICAL THINKING TO FEELINGS FOR GREATER EMOTIONAL INTELLIGENCE 151

CHAPTER 13: CONSTRUCTIVE CRITICISM AS ELEMENT OF GROWTH 154

CHAPTER 14: STRATEGIES GUARANTEED TO IMPROVE YOUR COMMUNICATION SKILLS 160

CHAPTER 15: AWAKENING YOUR INTUITION................ 176

CHAPTER 16: STRATEGIES TO HELP IMPROVE CRITICAL THINKING 180

CHAPTER 17: PHYSICAL INTUITION............................... 184

CHAPTER 18: NOT EVERYTHING REVOLVES AROUND YOU 187

CHAPTER 19: MARKERS OF A CRITICAL THINKER 196

CONCLUSION.. 203

Introduction

This book contains proven steps and strategies on how to become a successful critical thinker, to master problem solving and logical thinking.

The term critical thinking is used in a variety of topics for the purpose of explaining decision making, logical thinking and problem solving. For many, it is an elusive concept, yet, it can successfully be applied to solving a myriad of issues once it has been adequately applied to a situation. Critical thinking can be used in every aspect of life, including in business, personally and socially. With critical thinking, your ability to make well informed and reasonable decisions is a reality.

Critical thinking is layered in nature, with more than one-dimension present. This is because as you break down an issue or problem that you are dealing with, you begin to see it in various elements which are interrelated and come together as a whole. Think of the human body and the way that it functions. There is no simple answer to explain how you eat, breath, think and feel. If you try to understand the various elements that make you an operational human being, you will realize that you are functioning due to your digestive system, respiratory system, nervous system and so on. Then, you can go deeper into the contribution of each system to your overall well-being. This is what critical thinking embodies, looking at problem solving in a deeper way, that is logical and based on reasoning.

Critical thinking brings about excellent resolutions to problems, yet, it needs to be developed so that it can work, which requires you to have a sound strategy for success. Read on to find out how you can make critical thinking a part of your life, and how to improve your approach to problem solving and logical thinking.

Thanks again for downloading this book, I hope you enjoy it!

Chapter 1: Start Thinking

To start off, let's look at how much you are thinking in general. Let's face it, most of us spend most of our time in a mindless state. Whether we are going to work, perhaps even at work, cleaning, hanging out with friends, or doing whatever else, you might find that you are only thinking for a portion of this time. When you are thinking, you might find that you have trouble sorting through your thoughts or they are not relevant to the task at hand.

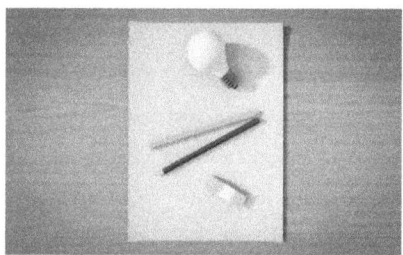

In this chapter, we'll talk about all the wasted time you have in your schedule that is used for mindless purposes. Some things do not require thinking. It is usually obvious which types of activities require thinking and which do not. If you spend time cleaning a stove, for example, you may have noticed that not much thinking is required here. You identify what needs to be done (scrubbing the surfaces and using cleaning materials to clear the mess), and you do it.

Another example is walking the dog. The dog needs to get some exercise (so do you), so you take it outside, put on its leash, and walk for a bit. Not much thinking here. However, there are a couple of strategies to change this wasted time into important critical thinking time. One aspect of this is that when there is context around these mindless tasks, it may be necessary to use critical thinking skills to make them easier or more efficient.

For example, you need to cook the pot roast at 1 PM and it will take until 5 PM to complete the cooking process. Should you schedule the cleaning time before or after this process? This depends on a couple of factors; you will need to address your schedule for the day and think about how long it takes to clean the stove, and what the effect of cleaning the stove will have on your physical and mental state, as well as coming up with a strategy to be an effective cleaner. The dog likes to be walked in the morning; if he is, he acts more relaxed throughout the day. You have a busy morning, so you must figure out a strategy to get the dog walked in the morning, as this is the optimal time to walk the dog while still addressing your needs and goals along the way.

Another strategy is to use scheduled thinking times for your mindless tasks. If you have a dog walk scheduled for 8 AM, for twenty minutes, find a way to incorporate some critical thinking into this time frame. For twenty minutes, you can sort through personal problems or things that have been holding you back. You can set yourself a schedule of thinking throughout the day that will help you to compartmentalize your cognitive tasks.

This is easier said than done; our tendency is to **slip into mindlessness**. You must face this tendency and use intentionality to overcome it.

What does this mean? It involves at least some measure of self-talk. Self-talk is what you say to yourself in your mind. It isn't a verbally "talking" to oneself, but rather self-directed thoughts characterizing our attitudes toward ourselves and our internal drives. Self-talk can go a little something like this: "I am starting to think about Betty at work. She is so annoying. Every day, when I go to get my coffee, it seems that she tries to get there before me so that she is assured a cup of coffee, even if I'm not." You want to shift this away from this type of thinking. Try to go down this route: "Betty usually arrives at the office at 9:30 AM. If I get to the office at 9 and make my own pot of coffee, I can avoid this problem altogether." Self-talk is necessary to route your mind away from the petty thoughts that it tends to gravitate toward and send you into a more productive headspace.

Self-talk is very important; it's a tool that will be very useful in solving problems and applying critical thinking skills. You can think of self-talk as one of the pillars of critical thinking. Each of us has "voices." This is not to say that we suffer from delusions or hallucinations, but rather that we have different ways of talking to ourselves in different moments. It can be helpful to identify and manage your self-talk by analyzing what you're saying to yourself. Some people have voices that tell them they are no good, or that they have a bunch of negative attributes that they must focus on.

These voices may sound something like this: "You are no good. You can't do that. You've never done that before; you will mess up if you try."

This is the first layer of self-talk that you must defeat before developing your ability for critical thinking. If you have these types of voices that speak to you, try to speak back. Tell them, "I am good enough. I know how to try new things. If there is something that I want to do that is just out of reach, it is possible to overcome my challenges and reach what I need." This voice that speaks back to the initial self-talk should be gentle and reasonable. It should keep in mind the realistic expectations that are appropriate for the moment.

It might take some time to identify the various voices of self-talk that are included in your psyche; for some, they are very difficult to disagree with. Some people have internalized these voices so much that they never question their self-talk. These kinds of people will have difficulty with critical thinking and problem-solving.

Being aware of oneself is an art and a science. Let's talk about both. Awareness can be an art because, sometimes, the way that you can express what is going on with you can't be summarized in words. Sometimes, it is a feeling, an image, or a habit of thinking. Awareness of yourself may come in fleeting moments; you may be gazing upon a beautiful vista when you realize that your mind is uncontrolled to the degree that you desire, and that moment can be beautiful. Being aware of oneself can come through artistic pursuits, such as writing or making art or music.

These activities can help you become more aware of the cognitive processes in your life as well as emotional processes. You can sort out the emotional from the cognitive and realize what needs to be shifted in your processing. There may be some great emotional block to getting your mind into critical thinking. Where could this have come from? It may have come from an overbearing parent, who pressured you when problem-solving situations were nigh. It could've come from a certain experience or association you have with whatever situation you are facing. Connecting with nature, people, or art can help you make connections and become aware of when you are thinking and when you are not.

If we think about becoming aware of oneself as a science, this brings to mind all kinds of ideas about how we can monitor our thinking. You may find it useful to write things down and keep lists. Many people like to write their thoughts out in different formats to become aware of what's going on in the mind. You can keep count of how many negative thoughts you have in a 12-hour period, for example.

This is a scientific formula-based way to do an "experiment" on yourself to gain insight. Here's a way you could format this experiment. For one week, without changing anything, just record your negative thoughts. Every time you have one, make a mark on a piece of paper. Have the paper divided into one section for each day of the week and try to specify when in the week these negative thoughts arose. At the end of the week, you will have a lot of data. Now comes the time to be a scientist. Go back through the week and try to describe what happened each day. Look for examples of times when you had excessive negative thoughts. You can find reasons and triggering situations in this method. Once you have identified the situations in which the negative thoughts arose, you can start to become aware of how your mind is working and what you need to do to eliminate those thoughts. For example, maybe you'll notice that every morning when you woke up, the chronic pain in your foot made you take a longer time eating breakfast. Then, your mind went into self-blame mode, thinking, "I am always late because of this stupid situation." You now have an objective perspective on this problem, and you can address your thinking appropriately.

Chapter 2: The Benefits Of Critical Thinking For You

There are basically three main benefits of critical thinking.

To Make Well-Versed Decisions

Making well-versed decisions is something that is very important in anyone's life. You need to make choices in almost everything on daily basis. The more you can use and apply knowledge and experiences, the better the decisions and choices you are going to make are.

To Understand Better

Your capability to understand is another important aspect in your life. You're open to an extensive selection of information you can get from media, internet, books, and other people.

Having an open mind to understand help you in coming up with opinions and making decisions. For instance, by reading and understanding about the positions of two political candidates you're going to have better decision in choosing which one you need to vote in election.

To Create and Discover New Things

People tend to create and discover new things by nature. We make beautiful art, amazing, music, and outstanding writings. We invent things like that will develop and make our lives easier on daily basis.

The people's ability to create and discover new things all requires critical thinking. It's an essential part of the entire process. There are choices and decisions in selecting a project to go through. Regardless of what you pursue, there are choices you have to make along the way.

Most of the situations that require making choices and decisions involve critical thinking. That's the reason why critical thinking can be defined as the capacity to create and perform well-versed decisions by capably using your lifetime understanding, knowledge, common sense, intellectual, instinct, feelings, and self-confidence.

Critical thinking needs the usage of strength of mind and introspection. The rewards you can get from it are the ability to finish projects quickly, great freedom, attain purposes, and solve problems with confidence.

Critical thinking is a skill, and it fortified by those who are willing to grow. Our brain is like its muscles that strengthen when use and withers when shunned.

Chapter 3: Problem Solving Strategies

Problem solving, in the Lazarus model, corresponds to the array of cognitive and behavioral responses designed to cope with the demands or opportunities perceived in the environment and the emotions that accompany this perception. Problem solving mechanisms are defined strictly in the transactional model as cognitive and behavioral efforts aimed at responding to the appreciation of the transaction between the person and the environment. It is necessary to clarify a point or a misunderstanding concerning problem solving, linked to the use of expressions such as "problem solving strategies," "Behavioral efforts,"... Problem solving can be conscious in the sense of intentional or intentional and even planned; but it can be as spontaneous, automatic, and out of consciousness; and it will most often be unconscious, that is, the individual does not know that he is reacting to stress, does not attribute his attitude to a particular transaction or does not understand that he is trying to manage a situation or an emotion. The unconscious character of problem solving does not, of course, refer to the psychological functioning in terms of psychic apparatus, even if some works have tried to articulate the problem solving with the mechanisms of defense.

Problem solving is by far the most studied theoretical contribution of the transactional model, for several reasons. In the first place, concepts close to problem solving existed prior to the introduction of the transactional model. In addition, defined as a set of cognitive and behavioral efforts, problem solving is a priori easier to measure than evaluations, internal and therefore not directly measurable. Finally, for Lazarus, problem solving is central to the process since it determines how the individual will act. In the short term, problem solving will influence the adaptation of the individual and, in the long run, will influence his well-being, the quality of his functioning, and his health.

It can be divided into two main functions: the regulation of emotional distress and the solution to the issues. Folkman and Lazarus analyze the problem solving strategies used in 1,300 stressful adult events and find that in 98% of cases, the two families of strategies are used (emotionally centered and centered on the problem). Holahan and Moos confirm this result with the avoidance problem solving dichotomy and extend it to a sample of patients followed for depressive disorders.

While both types of strategies are found in most situations, Folkman and Lazarus note that problem-focused strategies are over represented for potentially modifiable situations, while strategies focused on the regulation of emotions are over-represented when the situation seems immutable.

The Effectiveness Of Problem Solving

Is it better to deal with the problem or manage emotions? Folkman emphasizes that problem solving should not be confused with its effectiveness. This is a complex issue, and other features of the transaction, including the controllability of the situation, need to be considered. The so - called goodness of fit model of problem solving effectiveness hypothesis, introduced by Folkman, Schaefer, and Lazarus in 1979, proposes that the efficiency of problem solving is a function of a match between the controllability of an event and the problem solving strategies.

Strategies focused on the problem would be more appropriate when the event is controllable. If not, emotion - focused strategies would be more appropriate.

Although this idea is widely accepted in the literature, Masel, Terry, and Gribble obtain results tending to invalidate this hypothesis. They show that problem-focused strategies are effective when controllability is high. However, they also show that strategies focused on problem assessment and emotions favor relatively high and low levels of adjustment regardless of the controllability of the event.

Furthermore, the perceived effectiveness of problem - focused problem resolution strategies that focus on avoidance seems better than strategies based on expressing emotions and evaluating events positively. This influences the choice of strategies or even the change of strategies during the situation. Indeed, problem solving is influenced by feedback on the consequences of a strategy implemented. Upstream, the problem solving varies according to the evaluation of the constraint. Parkes and Long show that avoidance strategies are more used when the event is perceived as important. Holahan and Moos show that mobilized problem solving varies greatly depending on the intensity of the stressor. Endler,

Speer, Johnson, and Flett observe that the perception of controllability is a more relevant variable than objective controllability. Problem solving also depends on the chronicity of the constraint.

Although emotion-based problem solving strategies can be effective in reducing stress when conditions are appropriate, problem-based problem solving is generally considered the most useful and appropriate approach. Bandura notes that there are few stressful situations for which there would be absolutely nothing people can do to influence, change, or improve the situation. Moreover, the emotional impact of what is uncontrollable in situations can be diminished by effective management of aspects of the situation that are controllable.

Problem Solving and Defense Mechanism

Problem solving is a concept that has its origin in animal psychology (behavioral responses to control a threat) and in the psychology of the "I." In the latter trend, problem solving can be likened to the notion of defense mechanism, the two approaches being sometimes presented as complementary.

Psychoanalytic models develop the notion of defense mechanisms, the essential function of which is to regulate anxiety. In the field of stress, the works of Vaillant and Haan are the most cited. These authors have presented hierarchical approaches to adjustment processes in which problem solving represents the highest level of adaptation, whereas the most archaic processes correspond to defense mechanisms that are not well anchored in reality.

Haan's works, inspired by psychoanalytic and Piagetian thinking, articulate, in a hierarchical conception of the ego, complementary approaches:

The mode of problem solving consists of conscious and flexible attempts to regulate his emotions and his environment, the mode of defense consists of in unconscious and rigid mechanisms that aim essentially at the internal regulation of anxiety, whereas the so - called fragmentation mode refers to automatic and primary mechanisms, distorting reality and signing an ego failure. Otherwise expressed, the individual uses the modes of problem solving in his daily life, faced with constraints whose consequences he can regulate; the defenses intervene when the constraints are such that they imply psychic adjustments and the modes of fragmentation occur when the constraint is intolerable for the person.

The Problem Solving Styles

The problem solving styles correspond to the idea that there is common problem solving strategies used regardless of the stressful situations. This approach fits into a dispositional perspective that brings together the stable characteristics of the individual, especially the personality. It also responds to the difficulties of situational problem solving, a phenomenon that is by nature fluctuating and, therefore, difficult to measure. Situational problem solving scales have limited psychometric qualities, while problem solving style scales are stronger. Moreover, and this is the main experimental difficulty with these two approaches, the two types of measures are often poorly correlated.

In other words, the usual tendency to cope is only a poor predictor of the reactions adopted in a given situation. Also, problem solving styles and situational problem solving are often put in competition. Yet, both notions are relevant and reflect distinct aspects of the phenomenon. Putting them in competition may seem nonsense and be counterproductive in therapy. Indeed, problem solving is a concept that has developed knowledge about individual resources. For example, Vollrath, Alnæs, and Torgersen conducted a longitudinal study with patients who had access to psychiatry. They observe, over a period of 6 years, that the problem solving style centered on the problem or the search for social support is a predictor of a decrease in personality disorders while conversely emotionally focused problem solving styles are predictors of worsening disorders. As a result, clinicians will have an advantage in simultaneously assessing adjustment mechanisms in specific situations, as well as the tendency to preferentially use certain categories of problem solving.

Problem Solving Measurement

The 80s and 90s saw the emergence of numerous questionnaires to measure problem solving. Several particularly dense syntheses have highlighted the stakes involved in the development and use of these tools. These issues are fundamental, psychometric, and practical. They concern the very definition of problem solving as well as methodological approaches.

The definition of a scale depends on the problem in which the measurement is written. Questionnaires are either general or, and often are, domain or stress specific. Given that the research framework is set, the researcher, whose goal will be to collect the strategies employed by a person, must, beforehand, guide the person to identify one or more situations (stressors). O'Driscoll and Cooper note that some research focuses on previously identified and common stressors to all participants. The others allow each person the task of defining the stressors that it considers significant. Traditionally, this research has invited participants to focus on a recent situation that has been a constraint. The other authors set up close experiences in laboratory conditions. These studies most often result in questionnaires centered on a specific event or situation and, consequently, poorly adapted to the measurement of strategies in the event of chronic constraints.

Problem Solving Inventories

Aldwin and Revenson note that problem solving inventories are highly diverse in emotionally focused strategies and, by contrast, less variety in problem - centered strategies. They attribute this phenomenon to the items chosen to form the questionnaire. These, to be able to be relevant in quite numerous situations, exclude too specific strategies. De Ridder, O'Driscoll and Cooper, Parker and Endler, Stone, Greenberg, Kennedy-Moore, and Newman note that the items of the problem solving scales are not relevant for all the situations. The nature and diversity of the items obviously have a strong influence on the structure of the questionnaire.

This structure is usually specified by means of factual analyzes. There is no consensus on the number and nature of problem solving dimensions. Some teams focus on two major factors (problem - centered / emotion - centered, Lazarus and Folkman, 1984) or three general factors (Billings and Moos, 1981, Latack, 1986, Roger, Jarvis, and Najarian). 1993). The number of possibilities increases when the factorial analysis aims to reveal specific facets rather than rather synthetic factors, the same scale being able to lead to very different solutions according to the authors (Ingledew, Hardy, Cooper and Jemal, 1996; Latack and Havlovic, 1992, Lyne and Roger, 2000). There are also several classifications of problem solving strategies: distinguishing between cognitive strategies and behavioral strategies, opposing active problem solving and avoiding problem solving (Roth and Cohen, 1986) or distinguishing the social context or not from problem solving.

In summary, the construction of problem solving inventories can thus give rise to a general or specific scale, associated with exceptional events or chronic stressors, based on situations induced experimentally or recalled by the participant either freely or following precise instructions. It is understandable that faced with so many possibilities of definition, faced with such a diversity of the strategies evoked, and with so many methodological and theoretical choices for researchers, the scales are very diversified. Therefore, the clinician who wishes to use such a questionnaire must be vigilant about the development framework of this tool and question its validity in a sometimes different clinical setting.

Inductive Measurements

Some researchers wanted to deepen the situational nature of problem solving. O'Driscoll and Cooper highlight the interest of inductive problem solving measures and propose ecological alternatives. Stone and his collaborators proposed a protocol longitudinal with repeated measurements daily to study this aspect. Stone et al. (1998) show that there is a low correlation between environmental measures and retrospective measures, even when they are very short-term data (within 48 hours). More specifically, these authors find that the retrospective bias consists of a reduction of the cognitive component of problem solving in favor of the behavioral component. However, it can also be hypothesized that what is recalled from the strategies implemented by individuals corresponds to the strategies that individuals consider significant or effective.

Mayes, Johnson, and Sadri compared the variance explained by the situation to that explained by the personality. They conclude that both aspects are equally important. With a rigorous study, O'Brien and DeLongis also indicate that problem solving is predicted by personality as well as by situational characteristics. Above all, these authors highlight that the regression model is better when it combines these two sources of variation that are complementary. In this chapter, it is, therefore, necessary to explore the contribution of structural approaches in the context of stress by artificially splitting the negative and positive components.

Effective Negative and Neuroticism

Neuroticism is often defined as a stable tendency to experience negative effects such as fear, sadness, or anxiety. Costa and McCrae have found that people with high levels of neuroticism report a wide variety of somatic complaints. Watson and Clark, in 1984, propose to confuse different notions: trait anxiety, neuroticism, maladjustment (general maladjustment), and social desirability with the more synthetic notion of negative affectivity. One could distinguish negative affectivity, considered as a stable trait and affecting all areas of life, very conceptually close to neuroticism, and negative affectivity considered a state that would be a transient manifestation and expression in daily life. For Watson and Pennebaker, neuroticism (negative affectivity trait) and negative affectivity state are forms of distress whose expression is variable, ranging from a somatic complaint to unpleasant affective states.

Negative Affectivity and Problem Solving

The negative affectivity leads individuals to achieve a return proportionate tell of their past painful experiences. They would rate situations in everyday life as more frightening than people with low neuroticism (Watson and Hubbard, 1996). Larsen (1992) shows that the two evocations of symptoms, immediate and delayed (delay greater than 2 months), are only moderately inter-correlated and that negative affectivity is associated with delayed evocation. This author concludes that neuroticism intervenes at the recall stage and not at the encoding stage. When the recall period is low, Brown and Moskowitz, in 1997, do not observe this link between somatic complaints and neuroticism.

Between the assessment of life events and the evaluation of their outcome, Brief, Burke, George, Robinson, and Webster (1988), as well as Burke, Brief, and George (1993), obtain weaker connections when the negative affectivity is controlled.

Spector, Chen, and O'Connel have noted that the correlations between the hassle and their consequences are affected by negative affectivity. For Gunthert, Cohen, and Armeli (1999), the rise of neuroticism influences the different cognitive evaluations of transactions and leads to the implementation of problem solving strategies whose adaptive value is less.

Other authors, such as Hart (1999), point out that the negative affectivity, as the extraversion are connected to the tone of the reported experiences, problem solving mechanisms and well-being. High neuroticism is associated with inefficient forms of problem solving such as denial, behavioral and cognitive avoidance, or disengagement (Carver, Scheier and Weintraub, 1989; Scheier, Carver, and Bridges, 1994). If we consider negative affectivity from a situational and transitory point of view, we find that, under the influence of negative emotions, thoughts are less developed, alternatives of fewer solutions, and the person tends to avoid potentially negative information about his efforts to cope (Fredrickson, 2001). On the cognitive level, some have highlighted the deleterious role of dysphoric ruminations (Lyubomirsky and Nolen-Hoeksema, 1995).

The Endurance and Place Control

The negative affectivity and was not the only approach to personality development in connection with the problem solving. Watson and Hubbard (1996) are quite critical of the use of highly targeted measures such as hardiness or place of control. Watson and Hubbard consider that it is now more relevant to use conjointly a problem solving measure and an overall measure of personality. Suls, David and Harvey (1996) distinguish three periods concerning studies on the mechanisms of adaptation: the first generation, dominated by the psychoanalytic current, the second generation, which saw the emergence of the concept of problem solving process and its links with very targeted dispositional resources, and finally the third generation that links problem solving to the general attributes of personality.

The Five-Factor Model

The best-known factorial personality model is the five-factor model: neuroticism, extraversion, agreeableness, openness, and conscientiousness. Watson and Hubbard (1996) obtain well-defined results using this model of personality. Neuroticism is linked to passive problem solving strategies, while conscientiousness (adaptive) is associated with active strategies. The extraversion has a secondary role linked to specific strategies such as seeking social support. The'agreeableness is of a lesser interest as well as the opening. More specifically, Vollrath and Torgersen (2000) note that a typological approach may be interesting: people with low neuroticism and a high awareness score are the least likely vulnerable to stress while people with a high neurotic score and a low awareness score are the most vulnerable to stress, that is, they report more painful life events and more negative emotions.

The Dynamic Equilibrium Model

The dynamic equilibrium model has been proposed by Headey and Wearing (1989). These authors suggest that, in the face of the subjective well-being differences engendered by recent life events (less than two years old), the homeostatic function of personality (extraversion, neuroticism, and openness to experiences) is to bring well-being back to its level of origin. Hart, Wearing, and Headey (1995) suggest that personality traits largely determine the apprehension of life, the problem solving strategies used, and the level of well-being. In this approach, stress would be an abstract construct that would account for an imbalance in a complex system that integrates personality, environment, problem solving process, positive and negative experiences, and well - being (Hart, 1999). Spector, Zapf, Chen, and Frese, in 2000, put forward other propositions such as the hypothesis of sliding (drift hypothesis, Zapf, Dormann and Frese, 1996).

For individuals whose resources have been previously affected by strong pressure, this means moving towards increasingly restrictive perspectives. This idea is consistent with the finding that people with elevated neuroticism tend to experience a higher number of stressful life events (Suls, Green & Hillis, 1998). In a somewhat similar fashion, Hammen's model (Davila, Hammen, Burge, Paley, and Daley, 1995) suggests that people with depressive disorder induce stress due to their depressive state. These proposals are also echoed the assumptions'advanced amplification by the team' or the use of resources in the resource preservation theory.

Many authors have looked at the characteristics of a good life. More specifically, it is to understand the ways in which the individual can develop fully and interact optimally with his environment (Antonovsky, 1979; Maslow, 1954; Rogers,

1961). These works are experiencing a new impetus today. Seligman and Csikszentmihalyi (2000) propose a discipline to whole, positive psychology, one objective of which would be to break with the tendency of psychologists to focus on the repair of what is wrong, to extend the field, especially clinical, to the development of the positive aspects of life. Positive psychology is presented as the study of conditions and processes that conduce the flourishing or optimal functioning of individuals, masses, and organizations (Gable and Haidt, 2005).

This proposal is not new, and WHO, in its definition of health, has initiated this change for more than 50 years. The novelty lies in the current desire to study and promote practices of this type.

The Components of Well-Being

By definition, problem solving is centered on dysfunctional mechanisms, and problem-solving therapy is supposed to correct these difficulties. Positive psychology can shed additional light by explaining how problem solving can add to the optimal functioning of individuals. One of the central notions of positive psychology is subjective well-being (Diener, 1984), whose components are cognitive and emotional. This approach is the one that has led to the most important work in the field. More recently, Ryff and Keyes (1995) developed a strictly cognitive model in which well-being is conceived as a multidimensional whole.

However, this approach does not take into account the emotional components of well-being. Subjective Well-being (BES) is an individual assessment of one's own life as a whole (Diener, Sapyta, and Suh, 1998). For Diener (1984), research on subjective well-being aims to analyze how and why individuals live their lives positively. This notion is based on a set of cognitive and emotional dimensions. On the cognitive level, the satisfaction of life can be broken down into as many areas as the individual has investments and therefore constitutes a hierarchical structure.

Negative and Positive Emotions

In the same way, positive emotions and negative emotions can be broken down into simpler emotions constituting a hierarchical structure. The subjective well-being constitutes the higher level of this hierarchy. The hierarchization of the BES can be the object of bottom - up or top - down interpretations depending on whether it is considered respectively that it is the sequence of favorable events.

Evaluate Well-Being

The satisfaction of life is an essential cognitive assessment turned on existence in a global way. The best-known measure is the life satisfaction scale (Satisfaction With Life Scale; Diener, Emmons, Larsen & Griffin, 1985; Poppy, Diener, Colvin and Sandvik, 1991) composed type items on most plans; my life is almost ideal. Positive and negative emotions are two other major conceptualizations of BES. They can be measured with the help of questionnaires such as the PANAS (Positive and Negative Affect Schedule; Watson, Clark and Tellegen, 1988), but the 20 items of this scale are not strictly emotional, some (Determined, active, strong) involving a more complex system of latent variables. It is possible to evaluate the frequency of positive and negative affects to study well - being using the Emotional Values Measure (MVE, Antoine, Poinsot, and Congard, 2007), a tool derived from the work of Diener.

Zelenski and Larsen (2000), by measuring the emotions felt three times a day for a month, show that positive emotions dominate both in intensity and in frequency. Zautra, Reich, Davis, Potter, and Nicolson (2000) report among elderly and adult participants that the negative correlation between unpleasant and pleasant emotions is low for an all-round group of people and much higher when the group is composed of participants who undergo a life event (mourning, accident).

Van Eck, Nicolson, and Berkhof (1998) show that daily aversive events lead to an increase in negative affects and a decrease in positive emotions. The more these events are rated as unpleasant, the more important these changes are.

Well-Being and Problem Solving

For Seligman, Parks, and Steen (2004), it is possible to enhance well - being by stimulating engagement in activities, working on the meaning of life, but also by increasing the opportunities to experience life. positive emotions. Positive emotions can be oriented towards the past (gratitude and forgiveness), the present (pleasure and full awareness), and the future (hope and optimism). They counterbalance the effects of negative emotions at the physiological level (Ong and Allaire, 2005) and facilitate the use of adjusted problem solving (Folkman and Moskowitz, 2000, 2004). Positive emotions help to implement and manage resources (Tugade and Fredrickson, 2004) and accelerate recovery from stressful events

(Tugade, Fredrickson and Barrett, 2004). They facilitate thought flexibility and problem solving (Fredrickson and Branigan 2005, Isen, Daubman and Nowicki 1987). Positive emotions seem to have many advantages when dealing with information to deal with problems, including more effective decision-making, finer analysis of negative information, and more detailed and flexible apprehension of the situation (Aspinwall, 1998).

Chapter 4: Bias, Stereotypes, And Prejudice

Bias, stereotypes, and prejudicial attitudes are alive and well in every corner of the planet and they are not all negative. As you work your way through this chapter, keep in mind that some preconceived ideas or categorical groupings keep us safe. It's okay to be cautious around packs of stray dogs, and it's okay to never want to eat any type of oatmeal again after having a bad experience with just one serving fifteen years ago. However, as critical thinkers, we are going to commit some time and energy in exploring other biases and stereotypes held by ourselves and by other individuals and groups in order to determine how valid they are and whether or not they should be discarded in favor of looking at members of groups individually.

Personal Bias

Critical thinking helps us explore arguments with objectivity and minimal bias.

Because we are human, it may be impossible to remove all bias from our decision-making process. However, through reflection and practice, we are able to greatly reduce our biases by seeking to view people and ideas as objectively as possible so that we can form a fair judgment based upon the facts in front of us.

The more we practice our new skills of critical thought, the better able we will be to judge ideas based upon the facts we discover through our research. In addition, we will learn how our biases work to keep us within our comfort zone, which may not always be a good thing because remaining in our comfort zone often prevents us from growing.

In order to examine our own biases, we are going to have to actually think about the way that we think. Do you ever think about the way you think? This is an interesting question, isn't it? What events and educational experiences in your past have influenced the way you process information? Are your behaviors directed more by thought, or by emotion? Are you happy with your thought processes? Why or why not? What would you like to change about the way that you think? Think of bias as a way to categorize events, people, places, and things in order to understand them better. Not all bias is bad. For example, most of us are well aware that if we are in a public place and two men near us are speaking in loud voices and acting aggressively toward each other, it might be a good idea to move away from them because they could end up causing commotion in the immediate area. We may have learned this from being around aggressive people in the past, or we many have been told by our parents that if people around us are yelling and threatening each other, it is best to move away from them as quickly as possible.

Some of the biases you have, though, may be inaccurate and may preclude you from opportunities for growth. For example, if you have always told yourself that you are not smart enough to go to college, there is a good chance that you will never even take the time to pursue the possibility of furthering your education. In this situation, you will not know if you have the aptitude for college until you take a placement test, or at least sit down with an admissions counselor to learn more about the requirements necessary to attend college.

Other personal biases may be harmful because they have allowed you to treat others unfairly or inappropriately. If you are holding negative feelings toward others due to their race, their religion, their sexual orientation, their gender, or some other grouping, then you should probably spend some time reflecting on those negative feelings. For each negative stereotype, try to remember when you were first exposed to the idea that the group in question had some sort of negative connotation associated with it. Where were you when you first learned of the negative stereotype and when did you learn it? Who conveyed that message to you? How was the message conveyed? How has it been reinforced since you first learned of it? Why do you think the conveyor or conveyors of that negative stereotype shared it with you?

Once you have gathered as much information about the negative stereotype as possible, you will then have to reflect on its accuracy. How can you test to see if the stereotype is, in fact, valid? Who do you have to speak to in order to gauge its accuracy and what sort of questions must you get answered? What do you expect to learn as you do this sort of research? How will you feel if you discover that the stereotype is invalid? Will you share your findings with people in your world who hold the same stereotype? Why or why not? These are all important questions you will need to consider answering in order to do the work critical thinking requires regarding personal bias and stereotypical beliefs.

Despite what has been passed down from generation to generation, not all (fill in whatever category you wish here) are evil, lazy, immoral, weak, or stupid. Your new critical thinking skills require you to view people individually, as opposed to the way you viewed them as part of a group before.

Perhaps, at least some of the time, our prejudices and our negative stereotypes are not so much rooted in hatred as they are in fear. If you do not know any gay people, for example, it is easy to group them all into one category and refer to them as "fags," or "homos," or "dykes." It may be that at least some of us do this because we fear what we do not understand, and a lack of familiarity with the gay lifestyle or culture makes us afraid when we discuss them with others or see a group of them on the beach. However, if we ever actually meet gay people at work or through friends and then get a chance to know them as individuals, then the fear is dissipated and we are then forced to question our previously-held stereotype regarding homosexuality.

Other People's Bias

One of the most important skills you will learn as you develop as a critical thinker is that you will be able to detect biases in other people's arguments. This will help you make determinations about the validity of what they are saying. In order to understand other people's bias, let's look at an example from current events as I write this in the fall of 2016.

As this is being written, the 2016 United States presidential campaign is in its final stages with Republican presidential candidate Donald Trump running against Democrat candidate Hillary Clinton. Each have their own fervent supporters, despite the fact that both also have very high negative numbers (people who view them unfavorably) as well. Polls have consistently revealed throughout the past few weeks that while their favorability numbers have shifted a bit, the shifts have not been so large as to suggest major changes in support, or lack thereof, for either candidate. This is remarkable, especially because the media have exposed alleged behavior committed by both candidates that many thought would have damaged them.

The staunchness exhibited by many supporters of Donald Trump could be explained by their unabashed frustration and disgust with the status quo of the American political system as it currently operates, and many openly declare that they view Mr. Trump as a political outsider who cannot be bought and would work hard to "Make America Great Again." In addition, many of Mr. Trump's supporters have also stated that while they may not agree with everything Mr. Trump says or does, they will vote for him because they cannot stand the idea of Secretary Clinton being elected president.

It is not all that difficult to spot the bias in supporters of Mr. Trump as their motives for supporting him are discussed here. Some people will vote for him simply because he is a businessman who has had no experience running for or holding a political office previously and thus has had no opportunity to be corrupted by the system. In other words, they are not as concerned specifically about what he believes in as much as they are impressed by his business accomplishments and his lack of political experience.

Other supporters of Mr. Trump are advocating for his election because they are banking on the assumption that anyone would end up being a better president than Secretary Clinton, or that any Republican party candidate is always going to be a better choice than any Democrat candidate. In other words, they are not supporting Mr. Trump or the Republican party as much as they are advocating against Ms. Clinton, the Democrat party, or both.

On the other side of the campaign, Secretary Clinton also has her share of loyal supporters who believe that she is a better choice for the next president of the United States. Some people think that she would be the best candidate because of her experience as a first lady (she is the wife of former President Bill Clinton), and others believe her experience as a United States Senator from the State of New York, as well as her role as Secretary of State in President Barack Obama's administration, give her the credibility needed to be the next President of the United States. Another reason people may end up voting for Secretary Clinton is because she is the first woman ever to gain the nomination of a major political party and stands a real chance of becoming the first female president. And finally, it is important to note that there are people who, like the Trump supporters discussed in the previous paragraphs, will vote for Secretary Clinton not necessarily because they support her, but because they cannot stomach the idea of a Republican party president or Donald Trump as president.

All of the groups of potential voters discussed here are making assumptions about both candidates and some of those assumptions may turn out to be true. Others, though, will be impossible to know if they are true or not because only one of the candidates will be elected.

Both candidates are counting on their supporters who hold a bias toward them, as well as those supporters who hold a bias against their opponent, even though they may not completely agree with the bias held.

As we consider other people's biases, it is important to remember that, just like your own biases, they have been developed due to their own experiences and the information they have received through others over the course of their lives. It will do you no good to believe you can change someone's biases simply by telling him that they are incorrect, but over time, you may be able to influence the thinking patterns of others around you by demonstrating sound and systematic thought in a way that they can see the benefit of such a process.

Chapter 5: Guidance On Sound Reasoning And Textual Analysis

Critical Thinking and Sound Reasoning

In life, you will interact with other people when it comes to communication and exchanging ideas. At various times, you may differ with or agree with each other. Most often, your position on a given topic will depend on your innate preconceptions and beliefs. However, to develop as critical thinking, you do not just have to follow convention based on their face value. You could improve your critical thinking skills by evaluating said ideas and eliminating bias in your inferences. As a result, you intelligently choose what to accept and believe, and discard useless assumptions.

Therefore, apply the following reasoning methods to your various situations as and when needed:

Deductive Reasoning

Being an expert on deductive reasoning will require you to pay special attention to the premise of a given conclusion. Your grasp of its predisposing conditions will influence a given outcome. This type of reasoning also goes by the name logical reasoning.

Here is an example:

First premise: If plants can make their food, then I must be a ghost

Second premise: Photosynthesis allows plants to make their food

Conclusion: I am a ghost

Now, the validity of the premise is inconsequential to the reasoning process that derives your conclusion. You may disagree with a given proposition, but the deduction process that led to the outcome is still correct, however inconceivable it may be. In the example given, you may not agree that plants make their food, but you cannot discount the conclusion that I am a ghost. Your inference ends in a specific manner because the factors which influence it will support it to be that way. This reasoning method leads to conclusions that do not let you wander outside of the conditions presented to you. Your conclusions strictly follow the terms set by your previous premises. Deductive reasoning is associated with logical thinkers, for example, mathematicians and data managers. It is common in skills, which require abundant logical thinking, such as calculations.

Inductive Reasoning

Inductive reasoning allows you to make conclusions based on previous experience. A series of repetitive occurrences influence your reasoning process to come up with your specific inference. Your determination depends on your perceived high level of probability or likelihood.

Here is an example:

First premise: The stock prices have been trending upwards at the beginning of every third quarter since this company started

Second premise: This year's third quarter starts next month

This company's stock prices will go up next month

As you can see, we can conclude based on previous experience. This reasoning skill is crucial when predicting a future unknown based on past trends. As shown in the stock market example above, traders can make predictions on future stock movements based on already known past market trends. As long as the relevant past patterns maintain consistency, your predicted conclusions are, therefore, highly probable.

Abductive Reasoning

In this reasoning method, your conclusions will depend on the level of inter-relationship between available conditions. Here, you use your gut feeling to come up with your inference. You have a hunch that thing A has a relationship with thing B, and as a result, situation X has to be true. You come up with a probable conclusion by comparing observations that seem connected in your view. Your determination is, therefore, based on a hunch or an educated guess.

Here is an example:

First premise: Water freezes at tropical locations

Second premise: Gasoline turns into vapor in arctic locations

Conclusion: Water has a higher boiling point than gasoline (this becomes your hypothesis)

As you may notice, your conclusion may or may not be factually correct. However, to determine its factuality, your outcome will have to go through a validity test such as laboratory experimentation. You will find that nobody can fully agree or disagree with your inferences until he or she carries out a confirmation. Post-graduate university students, when presenting and defending the validity of their theses, use this reasoning method. It is common in scientific circles, especially when coming up with theories about a previously unknown subject. A scientific researcher will use the seeming similarities between his observations to propose a hypothesis. His hypothesis is then experimentally tested, and if found accurate, it becomes a theory through adoption.

Retroductive Reasoning

This reasoning method allows you to conclude based on already known factual conditions. You get to put forward a given inference to account for a series of known occurrences. For example, if A and B are present, then you expect to find C. In this case, the presence of C is conditional on A and B, and therefore, you have inverse reasoning. You almost seem to reason backward from a specific conclusion to confirm your suspicion of its contributing factors. This belief has its base on your previous experience and is slightly akin to inductive reasoning. However, the difference is that you do not have to predict an unknown future or heavily rely on probability. C is consequential as a result of A and B. Your conclusion serves almost like a confirmation of your hunch. You will use this reasoning trend as an experienced police detective when investigating crimes that you know follow a given pattern. You use clues and evidence to point you in a specific direction towards identifying suspects and their motives. Another application of this reasoning is in the health care system. Doctors will use your symptoms and signs to come up with a specific diagnosis. The health professionals know that certain patient symptoms are often indicative of a known malady. Since all human anatomy is similar, chances are the diagnosis will be correct.

In conclusion, sound reasoning is a great way to exercise your mind in the skill of abstract thinking. Getting your brain to draw intelligent conclusions based on a given set of premises is an ability consistent with good critical thinkers. Also, you can effectively defend or critically challenge a given position regarding a controversial subject based on proven sound reasoning skills.

Critical Thinking in Textual Analysis

From time to time, in our world of communication, you will encounter different types of text messages whose purpose is to convey specific information. You will come across news reports whose aim is to inform or fictional stories whose intention is to entertain. Myths and legends stimulate your imagination. Besides, you may encounter seemingly factual articles and opinion columns whose objectives are often subject to interpretation.

When gathering ideas or information from such written text, your final inference must match what the writer intended. However, if not, your understanding of the same article should have the capacity to query the validity of the implied conclusions. To achieve this ability, you will need to learn the skill of critical thinking in textual analysis. When applying this skill, you must always practice the following:

Read the material analytically

Critical reading involves understanding the content of the written information. You carefully and actively analyze the material as presented and try to see whether you know its premise. This reading method profoundly influences your comprehension of the specific message. However, you should be careful to read the text as it is and not as you would want it to be. Do not assume the intended meaning of the written message. This critical reading method would expose any ambiguity and passive text that would compromise your understanding. Therefore, to understand the written text truly, you need to apply your critical reading skills.

Think critically

Critical thinking is dependent on analytical reading. You can only draw conclusions based on what you have adequately understood. Your understanding is dependent on the clarity of the message; hence, the need for prior critical reading. Critical thinking involves challenging the assertions made by the text based on your opinions and understanding of the arguments presented. Do you agree or disagree with the writer's inference? Critical thinking enables you to conclude, which may or may not differ from the writer's intended purpose. In addition to a difference in opinions, your other findings may also depend on current conventions or universally accepted facts.

Be objective

When analyzing text, objectivity demands that you set aside your assumptions and inherent beliefs. You will need to completely abandon your notions and assumptions and read the material as presented by the author. A common misstep by most readers is assuming the author's intentions and meanings based on their own experience. This unacceptable practice is hugely subjective and results in a reader's bias. Your bias compromises objectivity as your critical reading is distorted.

As you know, this leads to poor analytical skills, which further affects your critical thinking down the line. Your ability to question the author's assertions independently becomes non-existent. To maintain an independent mind, you should always maintain objectivity.

Recognize the structure of the message

This skill allows you to see how the contents are being put together to achieve the author's intended objective. You can quickly surmise the flow of ideas within the author's stream of sentences and words used in the text. Another characteristic you would use to identify the structure is the use of examples by the author. You should find out if those examples are relevant to the point of the message.

You could conduct evidence-based scrutiny to determine the strengths of the author's illustrations. Do they distort the message or add to its relevance? How the paragraphs are arranged and spaced should allow you to move from one main idea to the next effortlessly. A good text analyzer would identify any shortcomings with the flow of ideas and the organization structure. Having this ability would enable you to offer criticism of the written material constructively, and provide suitable alternatives to the author. Doing this will further boost your critical reading skills.

Draw your inference

Inferences are the conclusions you derive from the material. This overall take-home message is what you come up with at the end of the whole text material. Therefore, as opposed to critical reading, this stage will involve critical thinking on your part. As mentioned earlier, your critical thinking skills come in handy when making assertions and inferences during this stage. You should try to visualize and have an overall mental picture of your understanding of the content. In addition to this big-picture view, you should tap into your emotions to find out how it made you feel.

Has the article left you emotionally changed from how you felt before reading it? What was the overall tone and mood of the article? Combining these two inputs, i.e., big mental picture and emotional implications, should allow you to make your inference independent of outside influence. Describe the material in your own words. Your ability to come up with a separate take-home message highly depends on your base knowledge. This fundamental skill is your application of objective and critical reading that is void of bias and assumptions.

Raise queries and challenges

First, identify the writer's conclusions. Once you come up with your inference, compare it to the author's findings. Do they match? Do you disagree with the author's conclusions? Your critical thinking skills, which have guided you this far, will allow you to argue for or against any conclusions. You can provide alternative counterclaims to those of the author. You may also have a different point of view using other stronger arguments.

Your ability to come up with valuable questions at the end of your reading is essential if you are to provide constructive criticism. The ability to offer criticism or counterclaims depends on your ability to formulate viable arguments that challenge the author's assertions and assumptions. During such challenges, you may imagine yourself as having a one on one debate with the author arguing for or against the inferred position.

Book critics often have an uncanny ability to offer counter-arguments even in the most unlikely scenarios. If you are considering such a career, then you should always possess a curious mind. Remember, you cannot challenge that which you do not understand, and you must always have an alternative if you disagree with a given inference.

How You Apply Sound Reasoning and Textual Analysis

Critical thinking in sound reasoning is a deliberate process that exercises your analytical mind. This activity is a process that improves your reasoning skills over time and expands your intrinsic knowledge. Critical thinking challenges your automatically accepted norms and assumptions. Your default beliefs and viewpoints may not necessarily be the universal truths you thought they were. In everyday life, your ability to decipher implied meanings, metaphors, analogies, or abstract concepts boosts your mental capacity. Besides, your sound knowledge improves through the continued application of deductive reasoning skills. Critical thinking allows you to defend your viewpoints using appropriate evidence or open your mind to previously unseen perspectives.

Critical thinking in the textual analysis is a useful skill when writing articles and opinion pieces based on factual references. You will want the reader to comprehensively understand your flow of ideas and eventually come to the same conclusion as you intended. On the other hand, book critics use this skill when reviewing article submissions and offering constructive criticisms. In higher education, you may use these skills in writing and effectively defending your specific thesis. This ability allows you to validate your viewpoints through challenging queries and counter-arguments.

To apply your critical thinking skills in your daily life effectively, consider doing the following:

Verify claims before concluding

This habit is vital, especially in this climate of fake news. You should always question the validity of seeming truths by verifying their validity. Always exercise caution before accepting any information being spewed by the media as absolute truth. You are encouraged to use multiple sources to verify the validity of any news article.

Interested parties that want to influence your opinions to their nefarious often use fake news for their benefit. Such parties will target your trust in the honesty of the media. Always rely on trusted media houses or known authentic news sources. Learn to question opinions and do not be hasty to accept ideas at face value. Remember to ask yourself whether an article is too good to be true, and if so, then it probably is.

Entertain differing opinions

Do not be rigid in your preconceptions. Be open to other various opinions. You should learn to consider the viewpoints that are different from your own seriously. Try to understand why others view a specific subject the way that they do. This simple action will open up your mind to the various possible angles of looking at a particular issue. Besides, your intrinsic knowledge on a subject expands beyond your previously rigid perspective. You broaden your horizon, and in certain situations, you may have a change in attitude.

However, if you still do not agree with a differing opinion, entertain it. This action will let you understand why others reason the way they do. As a result, you learn to live and coexist with tolerance. You may also find those specific aspects of their viewpoints align with your own. A little tinkering or tweaking such aspects converts what seemed like vast differences between people into a minor misunderstanding.

Evaluate the implications of your held perspective

You may expose the shortcomings of a held belief by challenging its potential consequences. Always try to consider the implications of your held viewpoint.

Rather than questioning a specific perspective, you could examine all its effects. For instance, views on subjective matters usually have contradicting implications. Such issues deal with differences in climate change, religion, and science. The following are examples of critical thinking processes that you may use to challenge the negative underlying implications:

In case you are a Muslim: What is your opinion on sharia law? What are your supporting arguments for jihad? Can you offer alternative options to violent jihad?

In case you deny science and believe creation: What is your opinion on DNA similarities between apes and humans? How do you explain all the various types of religion? What is your view of the big bang theory?

In case you deny climate change: How do you explain the rise in glacial melting currently experienced in the arctic ice shelf? What is your opinion on the increased intensity of extreme or adverse weather events experienced globally? Do you have a piece of advice on how to reduce the frequency and severity of the hurricanes you experience nowadays?

Resolve your differences with logic and evidence

Whenever you run into a difference in opinions, it is vital to strengthen your argument position using evidence and logical reasoning. Applying sound reasoning skills in cases of conflicting opinions will go a long way to prove your point, or weaken the opposing side position. Using everyday examples as evidence for your situation would make it easily relatable to the other's stand. Most of your differences are usually minor misunderstandings in specific aspects and not the whole premise. You should bolster your points using calm and deliberate explanations with abundant evidence in real life.

For instance, you can argue your position of rotating earth around a static sun against a mobile sun transiting across the sky. You may evidence the sun always rising from the east and setting in the west at regular time intervals. Also, using inductive reasoning based on weather and climate patterns, you can predict weather forecasts to disprove an opposing belief in rain gods. This resolution technique applies both ways also, i.e., if the evidence does not support your argument, then it is wise to reconsider your position.

Be open to change

You may be wrong in your long-held beliefs and assumptions. In such cases, you should be open to re-evaluating your perspective when presented with evidence to the contrary. To err is human and so you should be free to alter your viewpoint. This flexibility to change is useful whenever the evidence contradicts your views, or a confirmatory experiment disproves your hypothesis. It is advisable not to rely on many educated guesses. You may want to eliminate any of your beliefs that exist on a hunch.

As mentioned earlier, critical thinking is the skillful conceptualizing analysis and evaluation of information to form a judgment or conclusion. Critical thinking allows you to be open to receiving ideas and arguments. It examines logic and reasoning to form a judgment. Critical thinkers try to understand the information given by asking questions and examining the answers using logic and reasoning without jumping into conclusions. They do not just receive information and accept them, but they always search for the truth in the message given.

For critical thinking to be successful, we need to have certain skills such as listening, analysis, evaluation, and interpretation.

Chapter 6: Making Mental Models Work For You

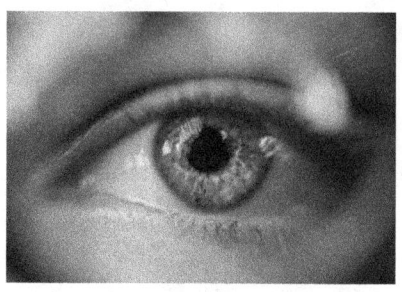

It is possible to go through life without ever broadening your mental model horizon, but it will be nearly impossible to make the choices that are thought out and perfectly assimilated for the situations and tasks that you face throughout your life. With these mental models, you will be able to broaden your horizons, allowing everything to work to its best ability. Your life, your career, and your choices will all fall into the perfect order if you are capable of relinquishing those modeling ideals that you created when you were just a child.

James Clear, author, entrepreneur, and photographer, explained the importance of broadening and expanding your mental modeling to improve your vision. He said that each one of our eyes can see images on their own. However, if you cover one of them up, you lose part of the image. Therefore, it is impossible to see an entire image or picture with only one eye open.

If you think about it, our mental models are giving us that psychological, internal picture of how the world works and how you work inside of it. If the world is constantly changing and evolving, wouldn't your need to change your mental modeling technique do the same? After all, you wouldn't critique the motor of an engine the same way you would critique a dish from a five-star restaurant; it would be an entirely different process altogether. In order to fully enlighten yourself on your options, you will have to put in some work. You will need to learn the fundamentals of fields and careers that don't really relate to you at all. If mental modeling comes from your own worldview, to broaden it, you will need to learn from people who have completely different views from you.

That mental picture that you create in your head needs a plethora of different perspectives to really pull from. The more perspectives you have opened yourself up to, the better the end picture will be. You will be able to think and process the world, ideas, and problems from a spectrum much broader than your own tiny bubble. This will allow you to fully understand the different avenues and choices that you have available to you.

In Mental Models by James Clear, he explains that creativity and creation usually happen at that moment ideas are being born. This is exactly why the appreciation and understanding for other modeling techniques and viewpoints is essential. When we are children, our lives are segmented. We learn life skills as a baby in large chunks of segmented time created by our parents. Each sector has some other objective.

When we reach school, that doesn't stop, going on until the moment we leave college for the last time. We pick our courses - specified segmentations of knowledge. However, when you enter the world, you find that the majority of highly successful people do not think in that segmented fashion; they have pulled together the different models, looked at different perspectives through life, and have put them all together in their minds. They are able to flow from one subject to the next, creating that connection that you usually wouldn't even realize was there.

Also, when you understand these mental models and how they can work with each other, you will be able to find ideas and solutions in those intersections. These are the ideas and theories that very few people will actually come up with. Only those able to freely flow from idea to idea will be capable of doing so. Although, you don't have to know every single one - just the main models originating from the primary sectors of life, such as biology, chemistry, physics, economics, philosophy, psychology, and mathematics. These are the basic building blocks to our lives and of our moving and evolving society.

Types of Mental Models and Principles of Each

There are very specific mental models used by some of the most famous people in the world, but those will be discussed later in the book. It is important to get a firm grasp on the most widely used and the broadest mental models used throughout life. These mental models can be applied to the business sector they are labeled with, but they can also be utilized in everyday life. Don't forget that mental models are not just for work, but for everything else in your life as well. Here are some of the most common mental models and how they can be implemented.

Common Knowledge

Common knowledge is used by everyone every day. It is the general information, the facts, and the understandings that almost everyone has. This mental model does not have to fit into any one specific category. It can be used across all subjects of life, from economics and entertainment, to math, science, and history. This information is always accepted as fact, usually because it is an idea of creation that almost everyone knows and can agree on. Some examples of these are the temperature water freezes, the rotation speed of the earth, how many inches there are in a foot, and so on and so forth.

The scientific method is a technique that is used in order to decide what is the real truth, and what is a societal construct or falsity aligned inside of common knowledge. This technique is primarily used in math, astronomy, physics, and the laws of nature. Within our judicial system, hearsay usually draws its facts based on common knowledge and, therefore, it is often excluded from evidence.

Diversification

This term is widely used in the world of finance. You probably have heard it spoken many times through life, especially in regards to investment portfolios. Diversification is the act of allocation of capital in a specific way to ultimately reduce exposure of any specific assets. There are several different techniques when it comes to diversification, but the main goal is to reduce risk.

Diversification as a mental model plays out with the investor. Understanding the market and the movement of it is key to successfully implementing the diversified investments. The size of diverse interactions within the financial account is limitless but has to be played out in just the right sequence in order to fully bring in the maximum amount of financial positives possible.

Game Theory

Game theory is applicable to a broad range of relations and is currently used as an umbrella term for the science of logical decision making in people, computers, and even animals. Game theory can be traced back to the 1930s, but the 50s were when it was extensively developed by scholars. In the 1970s, it was put into motion in biology but is now thought of as a very important tool in several different fields of study. There are multiple techniques, or types, of game theory, including the following:

Cooperative/non-cooperative

Zero sum/non-zero-sum

Simultaneous/sequential

Perfect and imperfect information

Combinatorial games

Infinitely long games

Discrete and continuous games

Differential games

Evolutionary game theory

Stochastic outcomes

Metagames

Pooling games

Mean field game theory

The games must always include specific elements. You need to have a player in the game, the actions available to them, the information available to them, and the payoff for the action. All of these can be internalized and thought about in a strategic mental view.

Anchoring Heuristic

Anchoring is used mostly in psychology, but it can also be a negative model if used without understanding the premise. Anchoring occurs when a decision has been brought to the table and the decider makes the choices based on one initial piece of information they have received. This is especially common in situations of emotion or stress.

Anchoring heuristic is the psychological heuristic where people assess probability.

They start with the anchor or the reference point that is given to them and then make changes and adjustments to it until they are able to reach a conclusion. The changes are usually very small, which gives the anchor a strong influence in the assessment. This heuristic was theorized by Daniel Kahneman and Amos Tversky, both of whom completed many studies on the subject.

The Illusion of Control

The Illusion of control is when a person makes a choice or solves a problem based on the idea that they have more control than they actually do over the event. Psychologist Ellen Langer named the theory, which is implemented by combining three main points of interest and evidence:

Lab experiments

Observed behavior in games of chance

Real-world behavior

From Langer's experiments, he drew the conclusion that people acted more in control when they were tested on skills rather than fact. These skills included choice, competition, familiarity, and outside stimuli. You can often find this type of behavior within institutions of gambling.

Tribalism

When it comes to mental models, the concept of tribalism has a great deal to do with loyalty. While it could be loyalty to their tribe or social group, it can also be any sort of loyalty used when making a choice or completing a project. When you use your brain to figure things out, you might find that, regardless of the world views you possess, you are likely to include your own world view and the world view of people very similar to you when making a decision or brainstorming ideas. This is a difficult thing to overcome, and it is a psychological aspect of mental modeling.

Working Backward

Working backward is also known as "backward chaining". This type of mental model is a thinking model used in computer systems. It is the act of working backward from the solution. Artificial intelligence systems use this type of model in order to compute outcomes for the data input into the system. This is the most often used method of reasoning and is utilized with inference from other rules and logical assumptions.

If a person were to use this model, they would have to be experienced in the issue they were looking to solve. It would be difficult to work your way back with a problem if you have no idea how to get there. This is both mathematical and psychological.

Homeostasis

Homeostasis is also known as "equilibrium", a term coined by Walter Bradford Cannon in 1926. However, the person to initially create the concept was French physiologist Claude Bernard almost

60 years beforehand. Bernard described the problem as such:

Homeostasis is the property of a system within an organism in which a variable, such as the concentration of a substance in solution, is actively regulated to remain very nearly constant. Examples of homeostasis include the regulation of body temperature, the pH of extracellular fluid, or the concentrations of sodium, potassium, and calcium ions, as well as that of glucose in the blood plasma, despite changes in the environment, diet, or level of activity. Each of these variables is controlled by a separate regulator or homeostatic mechanism, which, together, maintain life. Bernard, (1865)

This type of mental model is used in biology on a regular basis.

There are literally hundreds of other mental models out there, but we have highlighted some of the most used models. A few other models include the atomic theory, leverage, power laws, critical mass, relativity, and velocity. While using mental models, you must be thorough and knowledgeable. Sometimes, when in a hurry or in a frustrated mood, a cognitive bias can work its way up to the front of your mind.

Chapter 7: How To Learn The Basics Of Psychology

Psychology is one of the world's most popular subjects in college and university campuses, but that doesn't mean you have to pursue a psychology degree to know more about the human mind and behavior. There are many interesting ways to learn more about the human mind and actions now, such as completing a college course, signing up for a free online class, or using online resources to educate yourself.

For many, and for a good reason, psychology is a subject of interest. Through learning more about the fundamentals of the human mind and actions, people will gain a better understanding of themselves and others. Psychologists also play a vital role in the health care system by assisting people with mental health problems, administering psychotherapy, researching different treatment options, and advising patients on how to effectively manage their symptoms.

Introduction to Psychology

It's always a good idea to start with the basics when learning something new. Learn more about what the history of psychology is.

Spend some time learning more about what psychology is as well as the early history of the subject as you begin your investigation into this topic. The major topic that also covers nearly every introductory psychology class at the outset is a description of the many different branches of psychology.

Psychological research methodology How do scientists study human behavior? To think more about how and why people behave as they do, every psychology student must have a basic understanding of the research methods used by psychologists.

Even if you are not intending to become a research psychologist, reading more about how psychologists view the study of human behavior will give you a greater appreciation of the results that you will discover during your studies.

The scientific method and the psychology experiment cycle were important aspects of developing an understanding of how psychologists are studying the brain and actions.

Developmental Psychology

Throughout human history, not so long ago, most people believed that infants were just small adult copies. Researchers began to realize that childhood is a unique and important part of life only fairly recent. Developmental psychology is one of psychology's main subfields that focuses on all aspects of development and transition over the entire lifespan.

Developmental psychology research may seem easy; after all, we've all been through it. When you start exploring the subject, you will learn quickly that there is more to the creation thesis than you might have thought.

While reading about some of the main concepts of child development, recognizing some of the important issues and issues that affect developmental psychologists is also necessary. It involves the topic of age-old nature versus nurture, which reflects on the comparative roles of genetics and the environment.

Behavioral Psychology

Behavioral psychology is, during the 20th century, a significant school of thought that continues to be prominent today, also known as behaviorism. Many behavioral principles, including therapy, education, and animal training, are still widely used today.

Behaviorism may not be as dominant as it once was, but if you want to learn more about psychology, you still need to understand the basic principles of behavior.

Start by learning more about important concepts such as modern conditioning and conditioning for operators. Read more about the different types of reward and discipline in addition to knowing about these social coping strategies.

Important Psychology Theories and Theorists Some of the most prominent psychology theorists, including Freud, Erikson, and Piaget, have suggested theories to describe different aspects of creation, behavior, and other subjects. Although some hypotheses are no longer popular, researching the impact these ideas had on psychology is still important.

Some of the key concepts you must study include:

➤Freud's Theory of Psychosexual Behavior

➤Piaget's Theory of Psychological Development

➤Maslow's Hierarchy of Needs

➢ Kohlberg's Theory of Social Development

➢ Big 5 Theory of Personality

Personality Psychology

Psychology of personality is another major psychological topic of interest. As you learn more about psychology, you will find that some of the best-known theories of psychologists are focused on understanding how personality evolves.

Our personality is what makes us who we are. What factors affect the shape of our personalities? Is there a set temperament, or can it change?

It is important to concentrate on some of the key topics, such as characteristics and various personality disorders, to research personality.

Social Psychology

Why do people in large groups sometimes act differently? Social psychologists are trying to understand social behavior, including how we interact with others and how others influence our behavior.

Social psychology is a fascinating field that explores a wide range of social practices, including subjects such as the influence of the bystander, beliefs, and interpretation of the individual.

Basic Psychology Facts You Need to Know

For some people, a desire to pursue a career in the field stimulates an interest in psychology. Others may want to know more out of curiosity or because they're talking about visiting a health concern therapist. Whatever the cause, building a better understanding of issues such as sentiment, inspiration, intellect, affection, interaction, and research methods in many different areas of life will serve you well.

At first, psychology may seem like a huge and overwhelming field, but it may be easier to get started by learning a few basic facts. The following are just a few important things about this fascinating topic that you need to learn. Once you have a strong understanding of the basics, you'll be better prepared to explore various ways that psychology can help improve your daily life, health, and well-being.

There has not always been science as it has now. It is considered a relatively young discipline, although it has a short past a long history, as one eminent psychologist has explained.

While in the grand scheme of things, psychology may be a young subject, it has grown to play a tremendous role in today's world. Psychologists are working in hospitals, mental health clinics, schools, colleges, and institutions, government agencies, private enterprises, and private practice, undertaking a broad range of tasks and positions ranging from mental illness care to public health policy impact.

Psychology Relies on Scientific Methods

One of the most common myths of psychology is that it's just "common sense." The trouble with this is that psychological research has helped show that many of the things we believe are common sense are not valid at all. After all, if common sense were as common as people say it is, then people wouldn't engage in behaviors they know are bad for them like eating junk food or smoking.

Psychology depends on scientific methods to analyze problems and reach conclusions, unlike common sense. Scientists were able to discover relationships between different variables by using empirical methods. Psychologists use a range of techniques, including naturalistic analysis, tests, case studies, and questionnaires, to research the human mind and behavior.

Psychologists Approach Questions From Different Perspectives

It is possible to look at subjects and problems of psychology in various ways. Let's take as an example the issue of violence. Many psychologists may investigate how genetic causes lead to aggression, while others may analyze how factors such as family history, relationships, social pressure, and contextual variables affect violence.

Some of the main psychological perspectives include the following:

➢ Biological Perspective

➢ Cognitive Perspective

➢ Evolutionary Perspective

➢ Humanistic Perspective

Each perspective adds to a new dimension of understanding of the subject.

For example, consider that psychologists are trying to understand the multiple factors that contribute to harassment. Some scientists may look at how genes and the brain relate to this type of behavior from a biological perspective. Another counselor can take a psychological approach to look at the various ways the climate promotes harassment behaviors. Other researchers can take a social perspective and examine the potential impact of group pressure on bullying behaviors.

No one viewpoint is "right." It adds to how we interpret an issue and helps scientists to examine the various factors that lead to certain activities and seek multi-faceted approaches to combat problem actions and encourage better outcomes and healthy habits.

Psychiatry Is All Around You

Psychology is not just an academic subject that only resides in schools, research laboratories, and offices of mental health. Through everyday situations you can see the ideals of psychology all around you.

If you have a question, there is likely a psychiatrist who can assist there are many different types of psychologists; each focused on solving various types of word problems. For example, if your child has problems at school, you may be looking for advice from a school psychologist who specializes in helping children cope with educational, personal, psychological, and other issues. If you are concerned about an elderly parent or grandparent, you may want to seek advice from a developmental psychologist who is specially trained and knowledgeable about the aging process.

It helps to understand some of the different training and licensing requirements for different specialty areas to determine which professional is right for your needs. If you're looking to find a psychotherapist, reading more about which practitioners can provide therapy services may also be useful.

If you're talking about psychology majoring, then you should be happy to find out that there are a lot of career paths to choose from. Different career opportunities depend largely on your educational level and work experience, so it is important to research your chosen specialization area's required training and licensing requirements.

Psychologists Focus on Making Human Lives Better

The main goals of psychology are identified, illustrating, understanding, and changing human behavior. By contributing to our basic understanding of how people think, feel, and behave, some psychologists do this. In practical contexts, other therapists seek to address real-world problems that affect daily life.

And finally, many psychologists are dedicating their lives to helping people with psychological problems. Throughout hospitals, mental health centers, private practices, and other places, you can meet these professionals working to treat psychological disorders and provide psychotherapy for people from all walks of life.

Chapter 8: The Mindset

The mindset of a man is one of the important factors that determine a man's success or failure in life. It is fundamental in the interpretation of the things we see, the messages we receive, growth in life, beliefs, norms, ethics, our way of life and so on. The mindset is really a big deal. Consider the stages of growing-up and developing in life, where you start picking up different principles and beliefs from your environment and the people you interact with. If you grow up with your parents, you basically learn how to live and survive from their own beliefs, norms and way of life. You love everything they love and hate everything they hate. The moment you start going to school, you meet a new set of people with different beliefs, and then you start relating and comparing these beliefs and principles with what you have. You will end up developing your own set of principles, which explains why we all have different opinions and different ways of interpreting things.

Everything you have learned from your parent, teachers, neighbors, friends and your environment will be developed into a system of beliefs and principles. This is your own unique system that will be used to approach and interpret any situation you find yourself. Your way of life will differ from others, you have your own technique of approaching challenges and you make decisions and live your life based on your own system of principles and beliefs. This set of beliefs and principles of living and adapting are called your MINDSET.

Your mindset will help you organize the world around you and give meaning to any situation you find yourself. If you face a completely new challenge, you try to check your system of beliefs and see if you can relate it with what you have faced before. This is why your mindset is your "tool box", which has every tool and equipment needed to approach and interpret all the challenges that life brings to you.

Also, if you believe that success depends on skills and talent, you will find it difficult to adapt when you don't have the required skills or talent, and if your mindset or belief is that success depends on hard work and dedication, you will always thrive and try to adapt to any situation even when you don't have the skill sets.

Your mindset is your motivating factor in life. It explains the real meaning of positivity and negativity. Some people struggle with failure and negativity, while others survive and learn from the challenge. We all differ in the way we approach and deal with the same challenge, because we all have a distinct system of beliefs and principles.

Developing the perfect mindset from a young age is very important. This is why several psychological postulates suggest that parents and teachers are crucial in developing the perfect mindset for children. Parents must allow their wards to make decisions themselves, while teachers should explain how the brain works, so these children can have the sense of control over everything they do.

Your ability to control any situation determines the type of mindset that you have built over time. The perfect mindset boosts your motivation, improves you, teaches you how to learn from failure and teaches you how to hold to success. You see yourself growing and improving every day. For instance, remember the story of the hare and the tortoise? The hare was so confident and never imagine losing a race to the tortoise. He said he will win the race without running. He decided to take a nap during the race, while the tortoise just kept going. The tortoise knew his opponent was better than him, but he still believed he had a chance. He held on to his positive and growth belief that kept him confident and motivated. When the hare woke up, he started running as fast as he could, but he had already lost the race. The mindset is simply the perfect tool to achieve all your goals in life.

Before we get into the various ways that we can develop the perfect mindset that will allow us get rid of negativity, let us discuss the importance of the perfect mindset.

How powerful is the perfect mindset?

Your mindset controls everything you do in life and this is why your mindset is your life. Your life is something you must shape and control. You must always stay dedicated to ensuring that your life stays amazing and incredible. The following are the importance of the perfect mindset:

You own your life

The perfect mindset gives you the courage, passion and enthusiasm to take charge and control your life. You take responsibility for what you do and believe it will always bring positivity. You start to build success, good health and wealth using your own rules. Consider a quote by the great Bob Moawad on taking responsibility of your own life:

"The best day of your life is the one on which you decide your life is your own. No apologies or excuses. No one to lean on, rely on, or blame. The gift is yours — it is an amazing journey — and you alone are responsible for the quality of it. This is the day your life really begins."

The perfect mindset won't allow you don't blame anyone for your failures. You accept your own choice, behaviors, actions and decisions. If you fail, you start seeing failures or negativities as a lesson. This will help you become productive, especially at work and in your home. You become satisfied with everything that comes your way and you will never doubt yourself. Doubt is something that can stop you from moving forward, but the perfect mindset controls your doubt. You will never give up and you will always stay strong and positive.

The ability to discover yourself and your potential

The perfect mindset will not only allow you to take responsibility for your actions and doings, it will also allow you to see through yourself and see where you can reach.

Life is a journey where we are all allowed to grow, learn, love and live. If you don't discover yourself, you experience different forms of challenges that will make life difficult.

"Knowing yourself is the beginning of all wisdom." — Aristotle

The perfect mindset allows you to check your system of beliefs and principles and see if it is your true self. You won't just sit down and expect life to bring anything to you. You discover yourself, like you do everything you love. So tell me, how will you stay negative if you are doing what you love? How will you stay hungry if you are sure that food is coming? Why won't you stay productive and positive, if you are in love with what you are doing? Most people's lives are still not perfect and amazing, because they are yet to develop the perfect mindset.

Also, it may be difficult to discover yourself and what you can achieve, because self discovery is a whole journey on its own. Factors like environment, existing mindset, growth, age and time may affect your "self development" and "self discovery", but the right and perfect mindset get you started, focused and dedicated. You become so focused and determined to reach your potential. You will always hate what you do aside what you love. Your real self is the only thing that can bring you positive vibes, hope, courage, development and everything you need to overcome all life struggles.

Adopt the perfect mindset and discover your true self now! Take control of your own success right now!

Understand that life is a journey

People with the perfect mindset always see life as a journey with different stages and different challenges. This I must say is one of the most important things that we should know and understand about life.

Our system of beliefs and principles is really dangerous and should be built appropriately. If your mindset is not perfect, every challenge you experience in life will not be defined appropriately, the approach will be bad, the process of execution will be bad, and you will surely have a negative conclusion. With a bad conclusion, you see effects in the way you think, talk and make decisions.

The perfect mindset allows us to have the perfect plan. You work on your plan based on your courage and your dedication to doing what you love. You may execute the plan and fail, but it is alright to fail. What you need to do is avoid the same mistake that caused your initial failure. Repeat again till you have the maximum momentum, you will be unstoppable.

Continue to move to different stages of life with your courage, dedication and passion. Don't ever accept defeat. Don't give up. Understand that all the winners you have seen in life never quit. The moment you quit, you can never be a winner.

A project without phases will not be executed appropriately. If you move in the right direction, with exactly what you enjoy, you will reach and achieve your goals in life.

Life is a journey and it's about growing and changing and coming to terms with who and what you are and loving who and what you are. — Kelly McGillis

Every failure is a lesson

The mindset is so powerful that it allows you to understand that a failure is a lesson. Imagine putting a whole lot of cash on a project or business and it fails and you are told to accept this as a lesson. Well, it is actually a lesson!

The mistake we make is thinking about what the failure will actually bring to us. The moment you failed doesn't matter again, what matters is how you react to this failure, your composure, your desire and your dedication to stand up again.

Look at sportsmen; they understand that nobody remembers the second position, so they put everything to be the best. Sometimes they fail, but what matters to them is their reaction to this failure. The ones who reacted well will overcome the failure, while the ones who continue to think about the failure will remain in failure.

"I will persist until I succeed. Always will I take another step or stop my journey. If that is of no avail I will take another, and yet another. In truth, one step at a time is not too difficult. I know that small attempts, repeated, will complete any undertaking." — Og Mandino

With the perfect mindset, you have the confidence to control your life, discover yourself, understand that there are different phases of life; if you fail today, you will be successful one day. The lessons you learned from failures and your reactions are what you need to maintain and enjoy your success.

In the famous quote of the legendary inventor Thomas Edison, he said "Genius is one percent inspiration and ninety nine percent perspiration". He exemplified this quote when his laboratory got burnt on December 10, 1914. His lifelong researches, machineries and tools worth millions of dollars, and many other valuables got burnt to ashes. He didn't quit. He didn't blame anybody for this. He told The New York Times "I'm 67 years old, but I'll start again tomorrow". A.H. Wilson, who was his vice president and manager also told The New York Times, "We have only one thing to do, and that is to rebuild".

This is one of the several ways that a perfect mindset can help you live and remove negativities. What seemed hopeless failure may turn to an amazing success with little effort, dedication and persistence. People who persist regardless of the challenge or situation always end up succeeding and celebrating. The difficulties in your path are what makes the path. Never forget, within every difficulty or failure is an opportunity to improve your condition.

The perfect mindset won't let you delay the beginning or start of the things you love and desire, because of your fear of failure or fear of not reaching your goal. Failure is something that is common to the start of a new project. At most times that we start a new thing, we might lack the experience or find it difficult to adapt to the new situation. However, the start is the stepping stone for the success that is coming. If you fail in your first time, it is normal!

"A genius! For 37 years I've practiced fourteen hours a day, and now they call me a genius!" — Pablo Sarasate

When people quit because they experienced their first failure, negativity or disappointed, I always feel bad and troubled. Do you know what the new experience will bring you? Your failure is only a test (a preparation); you have to be 100 percent to survive a life filled with success. Hence, feel free to fail, take chances and make mistakes. That's how you learn and develop.

If you can believe that you can go wrong, you see yourself growing every day. You will be prepared and positive every time.

You will always get things done

The perfect mindset also teaches you the importance of getting things done and putting your best. This is another important part of life that can help you achieve your goals and stay positive.

You will grow the zeal and urge to make an impact and satisfy yourself. Although, you cannot be a perfectionist and sometimes the result may not favor you, but you will know that at least you gave your best and you did it.

Dani Alves a Brazilian footballer said in his biography "My coach said he doesn't need a 10.0 performance from me every game, because it is not possible, he just wants me to give him 7.0 every game, and I always try to achieve that".

You don't have to be 100 percent, because the real life won't allow you to be 100 percent. The only thing that a perfect system of beliefs and principles teaches you is how to get the job done. The moment you think you are perfect, you won't see any way to improve or grow. The perfect mindset teaches you to strive for the ability to continue to improve, not the ability to be perfect.

Chapter 9: Making Decisions Under Pressure

While the tips in the previous chapter are great for daily decision making, they often require you to take some time. What do you do if you have no time? What if you are under intense pressure to make a decision quickly? What if this is a stressful life-or-death situation?

Some of the hardest decisions we have to make under pressure have to do with our futures. Our health, our finances, our families, and other things that are deeply important to us call for our decision making. But these decisions create a massive amount of pressure because they are so dire to our survival and our future happiness.

Pressure can make decision making so much harder. But unfortunately, there will be times when you must make decisions under pressure. Life has an overwhelmingly high number of circumstances where decisions must be made quickly, with little time for deliberation and debate. You must learn how to not let pressure get to you and make you indecisive. How is this possible?

Making decisions under pressure calls for you to ignore the pressure. Let your mind stay strong, and don't melt or break under the intense pressure of time and urgency. Read on for tips on how to clear your mind and make a wise decision without the luxury of time.

How to Trust Your Gut

The most obvious answer is to trust your gut. But trusting your gut is not as simple as it sounds. If you are indecisive by Nature, then you obviously have issues just listening to your gut. You would not be reading this book if gut decisions were a skill that you can simply access whenever you need it.

Trusting your gut basically means listening to your own intuition. Everyone is inherently intuitive. But many people do not understand that there are three different types of intuition. Accessing your intuition may become easier if you learn which intuition to draw from. Also, keep in mind that pressure can make your mind work faster. Your intuition is a result of your mind performing at its peak, so your intuition is usually right.

Ordinary intuition is your basic gut instinct. It is your natural first choice. It is the voice in your head that says, "Do this, not that." There is usually no reasoning or thought behind this intuition. It simply seems to appear out of nowhere. In actuality, it does not appear from nowhere, but rather it emerges from complex thought processes and understanding that goes on in the deep subconscious of your mind. This is why your intuition is typically right.

If you ever hear this little voice speak up, it is wise to listen. Your mind might flood with doubt. "Is this really the right option? What about...?" you may ask yourself. But do not question your gut instinct. Always listen to it.

Strategic intuition is a little slower. It is just like ordinary intuition in that it will come to you out of nowhere, like a clear lightning flash, or a light bulb going off. But usually this intuition takes a while to occur. It is because the decision making is going on in the back of your mind, without your conscious involvement. You should also always follow what these flashes of insight tell you to do. This intuition is certainly enlightening, but it is not always useful when you are under the pressure of time.

Expert intuition arises when you are familiar with someone. This is the kind of intuition that might guide you in your career. You are trained and experienced in situations relating to your career, to the point where you are literally an expert. When a decision-making situation arises, you are prepared. You know exactly what decision to make based on your accumulated expertise. When you are experienced in something, listen to your expert intuition. You know more than you give yourself credit for. If your mind immediately retrieves a decision, go with that decision. Your subconscious has the appropriate knowledge to make the decision based on your experience and knowledge, without you having to spend time thinking.

Sometimes, you do not have a clear intuitive voice speak to you right away. When this happens, you should rely on either strategic intuition or expert intuition. But what happens if you don't have any expert intuition either, and you do not have time for strategic intuition to take place in the back of your mind? Then you do have to commit a little bit of conscious effort to the decision making process.

Commit to the Decision

Once you have realize that you have no idea what decision to make, you need to soundly and firmly commit to the process of making a decision within a certain period of time. This commitment helps anchor you to the decision making process so that you actually dedicate time and effort to the decision. You are not going to leave the decision up to fate or up to other people. You are the one who is going to make it.

Now you need to take some steps to make the best decision possible.

Know the Situation

Even when you are under pressure, it is a good idea to ask for a little time to get all the facts straight. You want to know the situation inside and out. You want all of the details. You do not need hours to gather all of the details, but at least take a few minutes to get to know the situation really well.

It is a good idea to ask questions that are designed to cull as much information as possible in a short period of time. Do not ask meandering questions. Rather, ask direct ones about the details that you know you need to make an informed decision.

Employ research if you must. What option is the best? You do not want to make the wrong decision, so you should not let pressure make you neglect to check your facts. However, remember to be a satisficer, not a maximizer. There is no point doing so much research that you confuse yourself. Find out what you need to know to make an informed choice and cut the research off there. Do not go overboard.

With all of the details in place, you are better able to make an informed and educated decision. Knowledge is power when it comes to decision making. Have all the knowledge you can gather to make a proper decision.

Prediction

You cannot predict the future, people say, and they are somewhat right. But with life experience comes a certain ability to recognize patterns and learn from the past. You are better able to predict the outcomes of your decisions than people give you credit for. You can usually have a reasonable prediction about what your different outcomes will be. Use your ability to predict outcomes to determine which decision will have the best results.

It is a good idea to not focus on the negative when predicting outcomes. You can bring a sense of doom into the decision-making process if you focus on which outcome will be worse. Instead, think of which outcome is better. Focus on the benefits and the pros rather than the harms and the cons.

Also, focus on the long-term. Some short-term strife may be better if it avoids long-term problems. Do not make a decision based solely on the short-term benefits that you can see. Use your knowledge of the decision to try to forecast far into the future. It is not always possible to understand the far-reaching implications of your decisions, so sometimes the short-term is all you have to work with. But at least try to keep your scope as long-term as possible.

Good leaders make decisions based on the far future. They understand that a decision that benefits only the short-term will create more problems to fix later on. It is far easier to prevent those problems by focusing on the long-term. Leaders employ strategic decision-making, where their decisions are designed to solve as many problems as possible. They see more than what is before them right now. Many people focus only on the short-term and instant gratification, and they despise good leaders for decisions that do not seem to be wise at first. Many people fail to realize that the short-term is not as important and that a larger strategy is in the works.

Keep this strategy in mind. Focus on the long-term over the short-term always. Do not worry about what other people see; if a decision creates short-term problems but benefits everyone more in the long-term, then make that decision, and deal with the consequences now rather than later. People may judge you and call you foolish, but they simply do not understand the greater good that you are concerning yourself with. There is wisdom to your decision that others cannot be expected to understand immediately.

Get Advice

Usually, it is advisable to make decisions on your own. Other opinions can only distract you and confuse you. However, at certain times, expert opinions and objective outside perspectives can be crucial. You sometimes need a second pair of eyes to help you see a situation in the proper perspective. This is why businesses often rely on outside consultants for advice on how to approach certain business and financial situations and dilemmas.

Ask people who are not biased by personal involvement in your decision. Ask experts, or objective friends. Really listen to and derive value from their input.

However, the opinion of an objective source is not always right. It can be helpful to ask people for input. But sometimes the reason that this is helpful is because it helps you see how right your own intuition is. If someone suggests a decision that does not jive well with your heart, then by all means, do not take the advice. You are not obligated to make a choice based on someone's input. The decision is still yours to make. Go with the choice that feels best to you. Be sure to always thank other parties for their help, however. You do not want anyone to feel unappreciated if you go against their advice, or they may not want to help you again in the future.

Run Risk Analysis

Do a very quick risk analysis in your head. Jot your thoughts down on a piece of paper if that helps. What are the biggest risks to each decision? Which risk can you live with? Think about this carefully, but a decision will probably become clear to you very quickly. There are some risks that you just cannot deal with. Then there are others that you can. You will know once you conduct a risk analysis.

Risk analysis does not have to take a long time. You can conduct one mentally very quickly and easily. Focus on only one decision at a time to prevent confusion. Writing it down really can make it easier to organize your thoughts, too, and to keep from forgetting key points that you come up with.

When thinking of risks, it helps to rate them. What is the likelihood of the risk? There is risk in everything. A comet might strike the earth and we will die in the subsequent apocalypse; there is always that risk lingering, I suppose. But what is the likelihood of that risk occurring and affecting your life? Not very high, probably. Some risks you think of are not at all likely to occur, while others are almost guaranteed. Rating the likelihood of risks helps you evaluate their level of impact and relevance.

Communicate

Communicate your thought process with the people who also involved in the decision. Good communication helps people understand where you are coming from and why you reached the decision that you did. It helps people prepare for the potential fallout from your decision. You will have a team of people ready to help you deal with the consequences of either decision that you make.

It is especially helpful to rely on your spouse or your family as your support team when it comes to major, stressful decisions. People make the mistake of thinking, "I don't want to worry my husband/wife about this. He/she has enough on his/her plate." But your spouse or family may wind up with even more on their plates if you do not communicate. Involve your family in your major decisions and communicate with them, especially if they will be affected by your decision. If a decision affects you, it will likely affect your loved ones somehow, too. You will find that their support is helpful and that it can alleviate some of your stress and worry.

De-Stress

Earlier, I mentioned an influential study on decision-making while under the influence of stress. The main finding of this study was that stress impairs your ability to make good decisions. Removing stress from the equation is helpful in reaching a satisfactory decision.

When faced with a decision, you need to remove stress. Unfortunately, decisions often put additional stress on you. It is best to remove any additional stress by removing yourself from the situation around you. Go somewhere quiet, even just the bathroom. Take a few moments to breathe deeply. You can even try using a stress ball or Chinese meditation balls to help still the racing thoughts in your mind. If you can take some time to really consider all of your options, then do so. But time is not always available, so make the best of the time that you do have. You can effectively remove stress from your mind in just a few minutes by yourself.

Chapter 10: Deal With A Problem

During your free time, pick one problem to deal with.

Find the problem's logic and identify its elements.

Know the problem, and analyze how it relates to your needs, purposes, and goals. State your chosen problem clearly.

Determine your options. What will be your action in the short term? What will be your action in the long term? Also, those predicaments beyond your control must be set aside.

Know your limitations concerning time, power, and money.

Act and apply your chosen options. Also, be ready to change your tactic and analysis as implications of your actions begin to emerge.

Develop your intellectual standards

Universal intellectual standards refer to precision, clarity, relevance, accuracy, depth, breadth, significance, and logicalness. Develop a heightened awareness with one of them each week.

Improve your intellectual standards include a lot of questioning. It's like questioning the importance and details of the things you're reading or hearing. Common questions to ask are the following:

Is the point logical or does it make sense?

Is it possible to express the same thought using a different angle?

Can you elaborate your point?

Is the point factual?

Can you discuss it in detail?

How can you tackle the complex or underlying issues in a point?

Is a point relevant to another issue?

Your intellectual standards shouldn't be limited in the superficial knowledge of statistics, depth of used words, and complex statement. Being critical is dissecting these points and questioning their essence in a deeper way.

Get rid of egocentric thinking

Egocentric thinking is having an automatic subconscious bias in favor of oneself. It is evident in human nature yet it is a detrimental form of thinking. Once you start to automatically determine egocentric thinking, you develop along the way an automatic system of self-reflection. Self-reflection is the key to getting rid of egocentric thinking.

Use self-reflection to get rid of egocentrism through these steps:

Recognize that you're egocentric. Accept that this is your way of thinking to give way to improving yourself. Thinking about it may be difficult, but recognition and acceptance are the first steps in overcoming egocentrism.

Egocentrism is something you can get rid of. This thinking is something that you acquired, which means you can still turn it around. However, remind yourself that getting rid of it may take some time. Be confident in the fact that you'll get there.

Stay motivated by thinking about the new and better you. As mentioned earlier, being a critical thinker is a sign of personal growth. The process of changing your thinking may be difficult, but always keep the future in mind for motivation.

Write an intellectual journal

Having an intellectual journal will help you keep track of your progress in improving your critical thinking. Self-assessment would be an easier task through reading your thoughts on a piece of paper. You can have journal entries on a daily or weekly basis.

Have a category for each of these four: situation, response, analysis, and assessment.

In the situation category, write down a situation that you care about. Describe why it affected your emotions. Focus on one at a time.

Write down your response. Be specific and exact in describing how you responded.

Analyze what you have written and determine what was exactly happening. Write it down.

Lastly, evaluate implications of the analysis. Did you learn anything from the situation? If given a chance, what could you have done differently towards the situation?

Ask questions

Questioning what is heard, read, or seen is one way of developing critical thinking. It was observed that when a toddler appears to be curious, he/she possesses a higher level of intelligence. And the benefits of curiosity don't only apply to toddlers; it also applies to us adults seeking improvement in our patterns of thinking.

It is different from being opinionated in an irrational matter. Having rational questions within us exercises our thinking. Agreeing to certain situations isn't wrong, but always agreeing is a big no. The next time you come across situations, search for self-kept questions. If you are able to answer it all by yourself, then it is a good thing. If not, ask, or search for the answer until you find it. After all, what is a question without an answer?

Ask questions and find answers through the following steps:

Use the questions mentioned in the "Develop your intellectual standards" section.

Dissect through the point. Get into the thought behind the point by digging deeper into the concept. Look at it in context and compare it with other points presented. See if the concept is logical, factual, interesting, and relevant.

Let answers come to you. You will start to unravel answers as you dissect through the point.

Search for additional insights. If you're still confused, look for additional insights by searching online or in other related documents.

Remember that asking question is fundamental in critical thinking. Don't be afraid to ask questions and find the answers through researching.

Chapter 11: The Art Of Pattern Recognition And Chunking

Apart from doodling, there are also other creative ways for people to improve their memory. As a matter of fact, there are endless ways to enhance a person's memory as there are always endless possibilities open to a creative person. With the help of creativity, we are able to come up with new and relatively exciting ways for us to be able to improve the way we remember and memorize things.

One of these creative memorization techniques is what is known as "pattern recognition." A person's memory, deductive reasoning, recall, and overall mental capacity are said to be excessively improved through our ability to recognize patterns and derive bigger ideas or extrapolate from them. This concept has made incredible advances in the realm of artificial intelligence possible, but most experts note that it plays a key role as well in enhancing one's own intelligence and even increase one's speed of thought. Simply put, pattern recognition allows us to be able to think faster since we become more adept in analyzing data and making out connections between various objects more quickly.

And there is even better news to this and that is that pattern recognition is actually a very easy skill to develop, only requiring a few simple exercises. This is because the skills required in pattern recognition are integrated in almost every aspect of our daily lives – gaming, problem solving, decision making, and simply life in general. The more complicated and more varied the patterns we become exposed to and we are able to recognize, the easier and faster it will be for us to develop new skills and enhance our abilities in pattern recognition. One of the simplest pattern recognition activities that most of us learn in school would be analyzing analogies. Analogies, no matter how simple, require us to find an association or connection between two seemingly different objects and use that connection to solve a given equation.

That same process of pattern recognition enables us to have a keener and better memory. This improvement in our brain capacity might as well be the demarcation line between us and monkeys, as suggested by Daniel Bor. He aimed to shed light on how our inherent ability in pattern recognition can be vital to our conscious awareness and our whole life as well as how it transcends to what makes human being human.

Numerous experiments even prior to Bor have consistently shown that the human brain can hold an average of 4 different things in its working memory. In comparison, monkeys are able to hold 3 or 4. This is where Bor discussed the concept of chunking – the concept which, according to him, makes the difference.

Chunking is described as a kind of "cognitive compression mechanism" in which humans break down huge pieces of information into smaller, more easily remembered chunks. These chunks make the process of memorization a simpler task as it paves way for easy processing of the various information we are exposed to. Bor explains this further by saying that chunking is a little like giving something your attention. You are trying to retain a certain amount of information with your thought processes. You also use preexisting information to make that new information more compact that means it's easier to learn.

To illustrate just how much chunking is of help to our memorization dilemmas, Bor gives us an unbelievable example revolving around a man who was able to use the process of chunking to massively expand his working memory's capacity. The man, with an average IQ and memory capacity, was put in a psychological experiment wherein the researchers would read to him a set of random digits. His task was to simply repeat the digits in the proper order that he heard them. If he is correct, the next set of digits would be one digit longer. But if he were wrong, the next set would be one digit shorter. This seems like a standard memory test at first, but this young man did the experiment for more than two years – about an hour each day for four days each week.

The result of his initial trial was pretty average and then he started getting better at it, remembering around seven digits in the sequence. This was a notable improvement considering most people only reach roughly 4 numbers. Towards the end of the experiment, around 20 or so months since he began, the young man was able to remember and repeat a set of 80 digits. Bor describes the result of the experiment by explaining that if for example, seven people were to tell you their telephone numbers in quick succession, it is likely that at the end of this, he would be able to retain those numbers and make a list of them without making a blunder.

The question, however, remains. How could a person with average intelligence be able to accomplish such an incredible task? Looking at Bor's response, this clearly shows how it is possible.

In the case cited, the man was a track runner. He was accustomed to thinking in numbers in seconds and minutes. For example, if he took 4 minutes and 21 seconds, he would be able to recall 421 easily. Thus, transferring this skill into his working environment, he would be able to remember more numbers. Then by clustering information within this numerical format, he was able to retain more information and up to 80 digits would easily be retained.

Now, how is this any helpful to our lives? Bor emphasizes that chunking is not only meant for us to excel in useless tasks. (Who needs to remember 80 digits anyway, right?) Chunking, as Bor points out, is part of what make us human. Chunking helps memory retention and that's the overall purpose of human consciousness after all.

Chunking also works in even the simplest of tasks. Say you're in your car, in a hurry, no pen and paper in sight, and your mom calls you to make a quick trip to the grocery and buy milk, oil, tomatoes, ham, eggs, and raisins. Problem is, you have no way of remembering all of those without writing them down. What do you do? Simple — and this is a trick that most people already do in their own time. You create an acronym out of the words you have to remember. In this case, you can opt for MOTHER. The letters that will make up the acronym you choose will serve as your chunks. So instead of trying to remember six words, you only have to remember one word (or six letters).

Chunking, however, is more than just about enabling us to recall and memorize things faster and easier. Bor argues that pattern recognition is also one of the best sources of human creativity. Humans, in their attempt to find patterns and connect disparate ideas and objects together, also develop the ability to use whatever pattern they find and make meaning out of it. Bor discusses that the ability to recognize patterns and remember them allows us to view the world with a wider perspective. He consistently suggests that practicing pattern recognition will feed our creativity in ways nothing else can.

In fact, reading this literature made me see that consciousness is part of chunking and that this is valuable because it means that what we retain is clearer and uses already existing criteria set in our minds to recognize new chunks of information more easily. That's pretty clever and is used by you on a regular basis, whether you are aware of it or not.

Ultimately, we live in a world where looking for patterns and signs within things has become a normal everyday act. Humans use such patterns to be able to make out or understand a blurry concept or even to make ideas more interesting. We use the patterns and the chunks we find to easily establish relationships between various things. Pattern recognition and chunking allows us to exhaust the capabilities of our brains. Simply put, these two concepts enhance our creative thinking by enabling us to search for the most interesting aspects of every dull and boring scenario – something which has become a powerful tool in forcing us to think more and use our imaginations to their fullest extent. Our quest for patterns and chunks in our lives opens up a whole new world of possibilities and wonder.

Chapter 12: Connecting Critical Thinking To Feelings For Greater Emotional Intelligence

Some people think that feelings are the reasons why people make wrong decisions, but that notion is incomplete. Unexamined emotions are among the reasons why people are likely to have the idea that it is alright to do things that they would probably regret later.

Why Are Your Emotions Important?

When you want to be a critical thinker, it does not mean that you have to shut yourself from emotions. Your feelings exist because of your experiences and your instinct, and these contribute to how you can gauge the validity of a particular case. You would not be able to decide to avoid a snake that you see in the grass without the feeling that you are scared of being bitten. That fear actually makes you capable of deciding to avoid a potentially dangerous situation.

At the same time, most of your values and beliefs are probably also based on your emotion. If you tend to argue on the side of wage increase, you probably know how it feels to make less money that is hardly enough to sustain your most vital needs. If you tend to lean towards the idea that people should stop doing the ALS Ice Bucket Challenge on Facebook, you may be feeling that it is quite unreasonable to do that since there are people suffering because of drought in Africa. Again, these are all based on feelings. You probably do not have physical evidence to support your beliefs, or that you may just be reacting from an observer's perspective, but it does not mean that you should not pay attention to what you feel.

Making the Connect

If you want to make sure that you fortify your emotional intelligence, make sure that you develop the ability to keep your emotions in check. You have to understand where that emotion is coming from — whether that is because of a previous experience or instinct, it proves that you have a reason why you feel that way.

Now, are the choices that your emotion is presenting you valid, or is the way that you feel just making you biased? Your emotions will always make you choose an easier option, but analyze if you are getting more rewards than drawbacks when you follow your heart.

When you analyze your emotion and the decisions that you make because of them, you understand yourself better and make better reasons why you choose to decide in a particular way. You do not simply say, "Just because." You are aware that you consciously made that decision, and that it is not just a spur-of-the-moment, instinctive decision. You provided reason to your emotion, and you are aware that you need to follow what your feelings tell you to do.

Chapter 13: Constructive Criticism As Element Of Growth

Productive analysis

A productive analysis is a way toward offering legitimate and well-contemplated sentiments about crafted by others, for the most part, including both positive and negative remarks, in an engaging way instead of an oppositional one. In community work, this sort of analysis is frequently an essential instrument in raising and keeping up execution measures. In light of the abuse of pessimistic, annoying analysis, a few people become guarded in any event when getting valuable reports given in the soul of a cooperative attitude. A useful study is bound to be acknowledged whether the research is centered around the beneficiary's work or conduct. That is, character issues must be dodged as much as is conceivable.

Four Key Elements for Offering Constructive Criticism Successfully

As a pioneer, one of your most essential jobs inside an association is giving direction to different individuals from the organization. It is vital for pioneers to experience circumstances in which they need to furnish a representative with valuable analysis. One concentrates even found that representatives acknowledge useful study since it can assist them with improving their activity execution. Giving this sort of direction can be a test, notwithstanding, as it is essential to figure out how to impart your aims without making individuals feel guarded or starting hatred. Luckily, there are a couple of thoughts that pioneers can remember to give their gathering better direction, helping everybody to work well.

Show the characteristics you need to find in others

It is significant, before moving toward any workers, about potential territories for conduct improvement, that you are not committing similar errors. Representatives are bound to tune in and regard a pioneer who offers essential input when that pioneer gives a living case of how to improve. For instance, if a specific worker has exhibited trouble remaining calm or overseeing undertakings inside a gathering, and their pioneer commits similar errors, the counsel about how to improve won't almost certainly be so generally welcomed or regarded.

Utilize genuine, explicit models

At the point when you have the discussion and offer your criticism, ensure you utilize real, watched guides to show the practices that you might want to see corrected. Talking about specific occurrences will give your evaluate unmistakably greater validity. It will likewise concentrate the discussion on particular occasions and approaches to determine them, as opposed to diving into character contrasts or noise, which isn't profitable.

Know not to utilize the words, 'consistently' or 'never.' These words can motivate cautious responses in individuals since they over-sum up. For instance, addressing a representative about their lateness by saying, "You are in every case late" will make them want to shield themselves against the allegation and discover times when they were not late. Saying instead, "I've seen that you have been late for as long as three days, this can be problematic for the group," will deliver an unmistakably progressively beneficial dialog.

Depict your response

As you progress through the discussion and disclose to the individual the conduct you watched, you likewise need to ensure they comprehend the effect of that conduct on you, others in their gathering, and the association all in all. For instance, an individual who battles to work in a gathering adequately ought to be shown how their practices are contributing horribly to everybody in the group.

As you progress through these means, it is essential to tell the individual that they have your help hand and that you are making an effort to chop them down, but instead help them develop as a superior representative and more grounded individual of the association. Remember this goal as you examine the circumstance and the possible outcome.

Allow the other individual to react

After you wrap up your perspective and the progressions you might want to see from your worker, allow them to respond. It is essential to recall that occasionally observations are not reality, or that there may have been outside conditions of which you didn't know.

Likewise, it enables the worker to have the chance to conceptualize ways that they may have the option to improve the circumstance pushing ahead. Make them a member in the discussion rather than only an audience and rouse them to finish on the talk.

Furnishing individuals with useful analysis can help colleagues issues that may ruin execution and collaboration. A significant piece of being a pioneer in figuring out how to control your association forward and that incorporates diminishing contrary practices or changing them into positive ones. Should circumstances emerge inside your gathering that request consideration, remember these plans to improve correspondence and have a productive discussion.

Chapter 14: Strategies Guaranteed To Improve Your Communication Skills

Tony Robbins, author, motivational speaker, and one of the most phenomenal and successful self-help thought-leaders, once said,

"To effectively communicate, we must realize that we are all different in the way we perceive the world and use this understanding as a guide to our communication with others."

Effective communication is paramount to making friends, influencing people, building healthy and happy relationships, mending strained bonds with loved ones, and winning people over when it comes to your professional life.

When you confidently and effectively put your message across and keenly listen to the other person, you build powerful social connections that open new doors of opportunities for you, help you create useful collaborations and move further in your professional and personal life.

Whether your aim is to get more clients, improve your relationship with loved ones, or impress the interviewers and land your dream job, you need to improve your interpersonal communication skills. When your communication skills are effective, it ensures that you communicate in a way that ensures others understand you just fine while you offer the same support in return.

Here are the most effective communication strategies that, when implemented, will revolutionize how you build interpersonal relationships:

#1: Know your audience

Whether you are going to have a one-on-one conversation with someone or presenting something before a crowd of 5000 people, you must know your audience in depth. This is crucial to achieving the desired outcome in your conversation or social interaction.

If you know that you are going to address an audience of college graduates aspiring to have thriving careers and wealthy lives, you will prepare your talk accordingly and use examples, success stories, and information that appeals to this specific audience and encourages them to take the desired call to action. On the other hand, if your audience is comprised of accomplished entrepreneurs from the IT industry, you would need to rephrase the same talk.

Before you prepare your talk or think of how to talk to someone if you are attending an event where you will have direct, personal interactions with people, make sure you have a basic understanding of who you will be talking to.

Here are few ways to go about this goal:

· If you are going to organize a workshop, present before your company's board of directors, or speak at a seminar or event, make sure to start by getting information about the audience. You can create an online registration form or conduct a survey requiring the potential participants to fill out basic information such as: age, gender, qualification, education, job or business designation, expectations from attending the respective event, or level of understanding of the subject under discussion.

· If you are going to a networking event focused on a particular subject, but you do not really know anyone, improve your knowledge of the subject. For instance, if you are going to be an attendee of a seminar on stress management, you should be aware of what stress is, what it does to your body and the basics of the topic. This way, if someone initiates a conversation with you once the main talk is over, you will not stay mute; you will have something meaningful to say.

· If you are attending an event/seminar/workshop, do your homework on the main speaker(s) and learn about his/her qualifications, expertise, and interests. His/her social media profile would be enough to give you that information.

· In cases when you are going to have a one-on-one conversation with someone you are trying to influence such as a potential investor, interviewer, business partner, your crush, or anyone else with whom you would like to build good rapport, find out more about that person as illustrated in the previous point.

· When you are going to talk to a loved one you would like to improve your relationship with, get an understanding of his/her emotional temperament and what influences him/her.

When you are well aware of your audience, you can easily devise a conversation pattern, speech or presentation (depending on the social engagement) that can effectively influence the other person.

#2: Pay attention to your body language

Body language is as important as the content of your conversation. Without you even uttering a word, it transmits your thoughts and emotions. When you are depressed, unconfident and unsure of what you are saying, your body language is likely to give that away.

To ensure you come off as a strong, confident, warm, and an authority figure when conversing with people or when presenting a topic, pay attention to your body language.

More precisely, you need to be proactive and work on the following tips:

· Don't slouch, hold your head down, close your limbs, or cross your arms over when sitting or standing as all these postures exhibit your lack of confidence. These 'low power poses' lower your testosterone levels, which consequently decreases your confidence and enthusiasm levels.

· When sitting, standing or moving through a room, keep your back straight, shoulders broad, head held high, hips open, feet at hip distance apart and arms on the sides or in the front. These 'high power poses' are mostly associated with high levels of testosterone. When your testosterone levels are high, you feel enthusiastic and confident and come off as a strong, influential person.

· Always maintain direct eye contact with your audience, looking directly at them every 5 to 10 seconds. If you are having a one-on-one conversation with someone, make sure your eye contact is not stern; direct eye contact every 10 to 15 seconds should be OK. While addressing a crowd of 3-10 people, occasionally maintain direct eye contact with every person every now and then. In case you are addressing a huge crowd, pick a few areas of focus and maintain eye contact with people in those areas every 20 seconds.

· Casually smile at your listener often so that you come off as a friendly, welcoming and understanding person.

· Use hand gestures on as-needed basis. If you are stressing a point, maybe thump your fist on the table or use an assertive voice.

· If you have enough room to move around, do not keep standing in one spot; pace around comfortably and confidently.

· When sitting, do not sit too stiffly in a chair, but do not lean too much into it as well. Sit straight and softly so that you maintain a nice posture and show your alertness.

· Nod when you need to show agreement with your audience.

· Do not fidget with your phone, watch or anything else; that displays your lack of interest in the conversation.

Becoming conscious of your body language will help you become conscious of how you sit, stand, and walk around at all times, which will help ensure that you never engage in low power poses.

#3: Speak when required and say what's required

Contrary to popular belief, speaking more does not make you come off as a knowledgeable and influential person. Yes, you need to speak when you are sure of something and to get your point across, but if you keep rambling on and on about something even if you are knowledgeable enough on the subject, you will annoy and bore your audience. To become a refined conversationalist, a general rule is to speak less and only when needed, and focus more on listening to others.

Every time you need to say something on a topic, think things through and speak only what is important. If you can make a point in 100 words, there is no need to go on about it for three full minutes.

Here are a few strategies that will help ensure you speak just enough words when needed:

· If you have a presentation/talk to give, prepare your talk in advance and carefully review it several times to ensure you do not speak more than what you need to on a certain point. If you are speaking to beginners on a topic, clearly explain a point in as much depth as possible keeping in mind the duration of the talk. If you are addressing a group of people who are experts on the topic, you need not give too much detail.

· When talking to someone on a one-on-one basis, be mindful of your thoughts and assess it before you vocalize it.

· If you are going to have a direct meeting with someone on an important professional or personal matter, prepare bullet points of the important points you wish to talk about and cycle through them a few times so that you don't miss out on them during the talk.

· When talking, pay attention to the facial expressions of the listener. If you see him/her twitching, fidgeting a lot, yawning, flinching their eyes or showing signs of agitation, stop talking because it is likely you are annoying, frustrating, boring or stressing out the listener.

When you start saying only what you need to say when you need to say it, you will effectively get your point across.

#4: Have command over what you say

There is a difference between an amateur speaker and a seasoned one: the former will not conduct a session or address a topic the way a seasoned speaker would and is likely to struggle a lot with effectively getting his/her message across and influencing the other person. To ensure you fall into the second category and build refined communication skills, always brush up your knowledge of a topic before addressing it.

Having command over a topic helps you come off as an authority on the subject, make certain that others pay heed to you, and win over people. This applies to both personal and professional interpersonal communication. If you want a group of people to buy a course you are selling, you must convince them of how it can serve them and help them achieve their goals.

Similarly, if you want your partner to agree to move to another city, you need to give him or her satisfactory and convincing explanation of how this move will be better for the both of you.

Here are some tips to improve your knowledge of things:

· Read up on the topic you wish to address before speaking on it.

· Listen to lectures, talks, and podcasts on diverse topics especially the ones related to the subject of your interest and work.

· Talk to knowledgeable people on the subject and absorb their wisdom by listening attentively.

· To strengthen your knowledge, revise what you know.

· Analyze a topic from as many angles as possible so that you get a better perspective of things; this will help you welcome different ideas from the audience/listeners, which ensures that you come off as an accepting listener.

- Be aware of the current affairs, both on the national and international level so when a certain topic comes up, you have something meaningful to say.

As your knowledge improves, you will talk well on a wide range of topics with ease and confidence, which will improve your communication skills.

#5: Pay attention

Paying attention to the person you are speaking with is one of those key strategies we cannot over emphasize enough. In his book, 'How to Win Friends and Influence People,' Dale Carnegie repeatedly talks about the importance of keenly and patiently listening to people and observing them very carefully.

People want to feel heard and offered empathy, love, and attention. That said, very few of us give that to our loved ones and even professional contacts. If you start paying attention to the people that listen to you, you will build better relational bonds and gradually master the art of interpersonal communication. This is particularly important for the one-on-one conversations.

While having a direct conversation with someone, pay attention to the following tips:

· When it is time for the other person to speak, give him/her a fair chance to speak and listen patiently without interrupting even for a second.

· Even if you have a valuable point to make or an urge to disagree to something the other person says, make mental or written notes of it and express them when he/she finishes speaking.

· Nod in agreement in places where you agree with the person. People need confirmation and validation of what they say so if you keep offering that to them in between the conversation, they will feel you are interested in the conversation and become drawn towards you.

· Do not fidget with anything while the person speaks; listen attentively.

- Ask interesting and meaningful questions related to the conversation so that the person feels and knows that you are listening with keen interest.

- Reiterate a point you wish for him/her to elaborate more on. For instance, if someone just told you he/she spent his/her childhood in Texas and you would like to know more about it, you could say, "Oh so you spent your early years in Texas. How was life there?" This encourages people to express their viewpoints and share their stories with you.

- To build good rapport with the person on the subconscious level, mimic his or her physical gestures or speaking style, a strategy called mirroring, which is an excellent technique you can use to connect better with someone. If the other person shakes his/her left leg, gently and casually start doing the same without the person noticing your move. If the person frequently uses a certain word in his or her talk, do the same. In a matter of minutes, you will be able to break the ice and make the person feel comfortable in your presence.

Implement these tips and tricks, and practice them consistently with different people until you master the art of communicating effectively with everyone.

Mastering the various strategies we have discussed in this chapter also ensures that you keep growing more confident with time.

Work on the next set of strategies discussed in the following chapter.

Chapter 15: Awakening Your Intuition

Every day we're bombarded with choices but most of the time we don't know whether we've made the right ones. How can we know for sure? How can we make smarter life decisions? How do we learn to trust ourselves? How do we develop our intuition? The following are the some of the most effective ways to harness the power of your intuition and be better at critical thinking situations.

Steps to Awaken Intuition

Make a Goal of Becoming More Aware of Your Intuition

Start by creating an intention to become more aware of your intuitions. Telling yourself that you're an intuitive individual and by actually believing it is a good way to begin. There's guidance from your inner being that you must learn to listen to. The information you receive from it is always present but you may overlook it all the time. The key is acknowledging it when it arises.

Synchronize Your Left and Right Brain

In order for you to synchronize both hemispheres for maximum functioning, begin executing daily habits using your non-dominant hand such as putting food in your mouth, opening drawers, or even when you're using your computer's mouse. Repetition is key.

Sharpen Each of Your Senses

We were taught about each of our five senses in school but never about the sixth which is intuition. But in order to master the sixth sense, the other five must be sharpened first. Exercise these senses until you can see, hear, smell, taste, and feel even without using their respective sensory organs.

Examples

Exercise your intuition by acknowledging the first response that you unconsciously came up with.

"Shall I have coffee or tea?" While you ask yourself this, you think of an image of a cup on a coaster. In a millisecond, you notice the black fluid in the cup. You can already taste the bittersweet tang of coffee in your mouth, but you cease this thought because when you look at the clock, it's already ten in the evening and you have to come to work earlier tomorrow. Give in to your intuition. Make that cup of coffee. After all, this is why they made decaf.

Keep an Intuition Diary

You're invited to a wedding but you don't have anything to wear. If you're a girl, you're torn between a white dress and a pink skirt that would match your pink blouse. If you're a guy, you would have to choose among your endless line of ties to match your single blue shirt. Finally, you succumb to your first choice. Write. It. Down. Record your intuition. When you look back on them, you realize you've actually made the right decision. Because wearing white when you're just a guest at a wedding is an insult and that polka-dotted tie just looks ridiculous.

You don't master these on the first try. These need patience and discipline. You may be good at ordering food from the menu or choosing paint colors for walls now, but with further practice, you could be making the best and most logical life decisions in the future using your intuition.

Chapter 16: Strategies To Help Improve Critical Thinking

Strategies for Improving Quick and Effective Decision Making

Utilizing the OODA Loop in Decision Making

Using the OODA loop that was utilized by the United States Air Force in air combat missions, we break down the loop into a four-stage decision making process:

Observe - note what the information says, gather from all sources possible

Orient - analyze your information to update your current situation

Decide - determine the correct path to meet your goal

Act - implement your decision as soon as possible

While in the observation mode, look to see how this information directly affects you and your department. Will this mean that you must cut employees? Do you need to redirect your resources? Is there any area that I predicted accurate results? Was I way off in my predictions somewhere?

While in the orientation mode, be aware of these things that influence your decision making process:

☐ Cultural heritage.

☐ Race and roles in your community.

☐ Past experience in a similar situation.

☐ New information not yet processed.

☐ Your personal ability to put aside prejudices.

☐ Your ability to analyze.

While in the decision mode, remember to be fluid. Look at each piece of information as it is gathered and add it to the current equation. Keep timely with the results of your situation. Don't base decisions on stale statistics.

In the action mode, start the process over again. This is a cycle, not a linear endpoint.

Systematic Decision Making

There are seven critical tools needed to effectively make decisions. Using these tools to assess your situation will assure that you have not overlooked important information needed for your final solution to the workplace problem.

1.Create an open environment where each contribution is valued and given the same attention.

2.Investigate the problem in detail to determine what is the originating issue, or if you are just examining the symptoms of the issue.

3. Brainstorm ideas in the group, and ask people to write solutions on pieces of paper that are read aloud to the group for consideration. Many times persons in a group can be hesitant to contribute for fear of ridicule. Having people write solutions on paper will bring out more

than one good idea for the project at hand.

4.Explore all the options for the feasibility, risks and outcomes of each scenario.

5.Select the best option for a solution. Try to reach a consensus within the group, but do not let the group turn into a popularity contest.

6.Evaluate the chosen solution. Look again at the risks, costs, feasibility, and projected outcomes. Look for unintended consequences.

7.Implement your solution and take action. Discuss the decision making process with those involved to attract more interest.

Chapter 17: Physical Intuition

They understand the world through acts and physical connection with the earth and its creatures.

Physical intuitive

This kind of intuitives understands the world through tangible or concrete evidences. They are close to the earth and the creatures which constitutes it. They tend to experience: the ability to identify vibrations from physical objects; a strong relationship with the natural world; the processing of the world through the senses; an the knowing of the fact that there is heaven here on earth.

The influence of a physical intuitive to the persons around him

They work to rescue earth creatures and protect the earth, and all its aspects. They aim to transform the world into a place of healing. Their objectives are to rescue animals and forests, and encourage others to do the same thing. They also: awaken the awareness of others regarding our sacred and divine planet; encourage the people to live using their five senses; and provide healing through the use of chiropractic, acupuncture, herbal medicine and traditional medicine.

Side effects of being a physically intuitive

Due to the fact that they are in-the-moment type of persons, they are more on action and less on speech. They find it hard to put spirituality into words, that is why, they prefer actions. They view spirituality as a concept or a theory and not a thing to include in a schedule or take the time to do it. They absorb physical energy so easily that they tend to experience stomach and lower organ diseases, sudden weight gain, chronic muscular and skeletal ailments and chronic arthritis, fatigue and fibromyalgia.

Staying healthy and well balanced-physical intuitive

In order to keep their body healthy, physical intuitives may need to take a full body scan each day. They should locate the areas where there are tense or sores. After locating, they must determine if they are the result of their own stress or the stress of others. Upon knowing the source of stress, it can now be released. Herbal medicine, chiropractic work, homeopathy and massage therapy works well with physical intuitives.

How to make the most out of being a physical intuitive

They tend to believe that they are not into deep intuition, because their way of processing, using actions and touch, seemed to be normal and common to a huge number of people. Yet, their power is not confined to actions and touch, but also the instinctive knowing of the creatures and the earth itself, who needed help. They can be an inspiration to others, if they will embrace the gift given to them.

Chapter 18: Not Everything Revolves Around You

So far we have focused on talking about your own personal feelings, how you respond to them, working towards your goals, and we have said very little about those around you. Of course, I told you how negative actions you take can affect others, but we have not discussed the feelings of other people very much. You have probably guessed that we will now talk about empathy, that word that we may have learned as little children, but that has so much power and meaning.

The first thing that comes to mind when you talk about empathy can be a phrase such as "putting yourself in someone else's shoes" or something similar. What these expressions or thoughts want to express is that you must try to understand the circumstances that made a person who he or she is. I think I've said this before, but we're all different, we're all constantly changing, and we all need different things in our lives.

Empathy does not require you to know certain things in advance, we cannot know everything a person has experienced, all the current circumstances of his life, etc. For example, asking someone about his father or mother to find out that they died some time ago . You may feel sad immediately, partly because you care about the person, but you also feel that way because you think it will bring acid memories to her; it is at this last point that you feel empathy, you share sadness and concern that you did not have in an attempt to let the other person know that you care about her, that you are trying to understand her feelings.

You can probably survive by communicating as little as possible with others, but you would at least need the basic skills of empathy for those interactions, at least to know if the circumstances require you to be in a certain way compared to others acts. It would most likely be inappropriate to tell a joke about cancer if someone who listens has the disease or has recently lost it to someone unless you already understand the person and know he would like it.

If you are emphatic, pay close attention to the people you are in contact with, the current environment, every detail (no matter how small) that you think might have an effect on a person's emotions. It is an indispensable tool for people in certain jobs, especially for people who need human interaction, such as doctors, teachers, sales people.

Why is it so important to be explicit about these lines? Well, because the relationship between the user and the service provider is based on trust. If you go to a fast food restaurant and the cashier looks like he hates his job and just wants to get out of there, this will probably ruin the mood you had and you won't enjoy your meal that much. But if the employee receives you with a smile, tells you about their specials for the day, pays attention to what you want, then you will also be happy and probably come back another time (and believe me, restaurants need us back to them).

The best actors must also be very emphatic, at least when it comes to the interpretation of their characters. They must delve into the writers 'or narrators' descriptions and they must do their best to think like the character would. Are they playing someone who has just fallen in love? Maybe a person who receives a puppy the way she had when she was a baby, what emotions would that show? You may think that I jumped all the way out of the subject here, wasn't I talking about how empathy was to other people? The actors (mostly) interpret fictional characters with whom they have not interacted! Well, that's true, but this is because we can divide empathy into different kinds.

In this case, when we talk about how we should feel when figuring out what the other person feels or thinks, when we are influenced by the same emotions that the other person exhibits, we feel affective empathy. When we try to understand and / or accept the perspectives of another, or why they feel in a certain way, we are dealing with cognitive empathy in that case. In this way, even if he is dealing with an imaginary character, an actor can still use cognitive empathy to understand how the character would feel based on the context of the story, and in this way he can act accordingly.

The lack of cognitive or affective empathy, in whole or in part, is related to various mental disorders such as psychopathy, autism, schizophrenia, narcissism, etc. People suffering from these disorders may find it difficult to fit into the world, or they can even develop cruel behavior such as in the case of psychopaths. Just as empathy can be used to understand others and try to feel sorry for them, it can also be used to harm them by taking advantage of knowing and understanding what they feel.

Empathy is not only useful to deal with the emotional state of other people, it is also useful to help you determine the needs of the people you work with, and the needs of one of us are very diverse. For example, if you work as a waiter, you must be able to identify incoming customers in your restaurant and after you have offered them the menu, you must wait until they are ready; however, this can be a very difficult part. You can either be really pushy and come back to the table every minute and ask if they are ready to order, then you will put pressure on your customers to order, which can make them feel uncomfortable or irritated. Maybe you decide to wait half an hour to find out that people left while they waited too long for you to come back. A good waiter will not be intrusive or neglect his customers for too long, they will continue with their duties, but will pay as much attention as possible to their customers. For example, if the waiter sees that the people at the table are having a heated discussion, it is best not to approach at that moment.

When he sees the customers' menu on the table, he can see it as a sign that they are ready to order. If some time has passed and the customers are still looking at the menu, they may already know what they will order, but they will view the list of deserts (I am guilty of this) so that he can approach and ask if they know what they want.

We have begun to discuss needs, but we not only have physical needs, we also have needs with regard to our capabilities, our goals. For now, let's leave the restaurant and go to a classroom. Being a teacher can be simple: you can participate, give any number of lectures you need until the bell rings (taking into account the approved course material), and go home, view what you will teach tomorrow and assess your students' homework with a red pen that marks right or wrong. However, this is not a very good teacher. Imagine giving a mathematics lesson in primary school. You try to explain it, while most (or all) of your students are completely bored; that's why you have to get their attention somehow, and there are plenty of ways to do this. Some teachers decide to be strict and let the students know that they do not allow disturbances in their class. Other teachers can choose to make their class more fun, to do their best to attract the attention and inquisitiveness of the students. But regardless of any method that teachers decide to use, they must be alert to their students. If the strict teacher notices that their students are confused about a topic, then they will have to explain it again, with more examples, try to understand it easier this time, and they may even suggest additional sessions for those children who are still struggling with to learn. The fun teacher must do the same: they must analyze whether their methods and activities, in addition to being fun, really help their students to learn. Every student will be different, and the teacher should be able to notice which children have more desire and ability to learn (and try to continue to cultivate those skills), and those who have difficulty learning (and try to find ways together with them) they can learn). If a teacher only focuses on demanding excellence from a few exceptional students in their class, the other children will start to get bored, sad, possibly angry, because they can't keep up. If a teacher only pays attention to those students who are behind the class schedule, the children who have understood the subject will also get bored with the class, and it may even reduce their desire to learn and get better.

Empathy therefore requires attention to our environment. It requires that we keep an eye on what other people feel and what they may need from us. Is it a good service that they expect from us? Or maybe they need help to develop their skills? Do they want us to raise their minds in some way? Maybe they just want us to listen so that we can provide objective advice? We can all and often will have the answers wrong, but people will find that we do our best to try to understand them, and that is also valuable.

Chapter 19: Markers Of A Critical Thinker

Now that you are aware of how to improve your critical thinking skills, you are well on your way to becoming a better critical thinker. As you endeavor to improve your skills, there are some markers to lookout for to know how you are doing.

Critical thinkers:

Seek To Justify Their Beliefs

Critical thinkers do not accept information at face value; they do not believe something just because others believe it. Instead, they seek to justify their decisions and beliefs. They look at hypotheses and seek alternative hypotheses in search of answers. They seek explanations and make conclusions based on evidence and facts.

Critical thinkers strive to soak up information on subjects they are discussing. They look at several points of views and ensure that they give others a chance to express their viewpoints. Aim to develop this skill.

Judge the Credibility of Sources

Critical thinkers are good at judging the credibility of sources because they rely on information to make good decisions. Faulty information can change the outcome of decisions. Critical thinkers are well aware of this.

They use various factors to judge the credibility of sources to ensure that the information they receive draws on facts and evidence. Critical thinkers check expertise, reputation, and the procedures used by sources. They do not look at only one source; they do research on a variety of sources and check for agreement and disagreements. They also look at the reasons given in support of an argument.

Proceed In an Organized Manner

Critical thinkers strive to organize their thoughts and their information well before they present it to others. They are good at problem solving because they follow problem-solving steps.

They refrain from panicking when there is a problem. They know that panicking only seeks to make the situation worse. Instead of overreacting, they take stock of a situation, determine the problem, and look for ways to solve the problem. They also determine who will be responsible for carrying out which action and how they will evaluate the implementation process.

Clearly Present Their Position

Critical thinkers are interested in finding the underlying cause of a problem or issue; they want to learn the truth of whatever situation they are dealing with. They are not concerned with 'looking good' in front of others. They are also not concerned with making others look good by distorting information.

Critical thinkers ensure that they present a position with honesty. They are clear in their delivery. They ensure that their audience knows their intended meaning.

They discuss the issue at hand, giving information, answering questions, and offering reasons. However, they do not pretend that they know it all; they are aware that they have limited beliefs and that they can learn something from listening to others.

Protect the Dignity of Others

Critical thinkers are good at presenting their point of view and analyzing the view of others. They are knowledgeable and confident in what they are saying. However, this does not make them arrogant. Critical thinkers do not lord it over others. They take care to preserve the dignity of others.

Critical thinkers also consider the feelings of others. They allow others to express their views. They consider the degree of sophistication and the level of knowledge that others possess and refrain from being intimidating. Critical thinkers can present the same information to people of all ages. They know how to adapt their presentation so that everyone in their audience can grasp the meaning of the topic in discussion.

Focus On Questions and Answers

Critical thinkers are good at asking questions, seeking answers, and giving answers. Critical thinking relies on information. If you want to get information, you need to ask questions.

Critical thinkers formulate the questions they want to ask, and have certain criteria when judging received answers. If an answer does not cover all the issues raised, they ask further questions or seek clarification. Critical thinkers do not ask questions for the sake of asking questions. Instead, they keep in mind the situation under discussion and ask questions relevant to the situation.

Engage In Observation

Critical thinkers hone their observation skills because they know that they can derive a lot of information from observing people and situations. They not only listen to what is being said, they also observe the body language of the speaker to determine what is not being said.

Critical thinkers are adept at judging observation reports made by others. They determine whether the author of the report was reporting hearsay or firsthand observation. They determine whether someone else can corroborate the information given in the report. They also check things such as the language used, and the lapsed time between the observation and the report writing. Human beings tend to show their bias through language. They also tend to forget details as time elapses. Critical thinkers consider such things when judging reports.

Seek clarification

One thing critical thinkers are good at is seeking clarification. Many times, sources of information neglect to provide all the details needed to reach a decision. Critical thinkers are interested in the facts and main points. They ask questions and paraphrase in order to determine whether they have a clear picture of the situation. Critical thinkers are adept at seeking clarification; they are also adept at clarifying their points. They give definitions, explanations, facts, illustrations, and answer questions raised to ensure that everyone understands the topic in discussion.

Analyze Arguments

Critical thinkers are good at analyzing arguments. Information alone does not make one a critical thinker. You need to know what the information means. Critical thinkers seek both stated and unstated reasons when searching for answers.

They view the structure of the argument, summarize the main points, and identify the conclusions. Critical thinkers decipher relevant and irrelevant information. They can also know when a discussion is getting out of hand. They employ strategies to bring the discussion back on track and move the discussion forward.

Conclusion

Thank you again for downloading this book!

I hope this book was able to help you to improve your critical thinking skills.

The next step is to apply the strategies and techniques that you have learned in this book.

Critical thinking has often been misunderstood in various ways. The largest misunderstanding comes in believing that critical thinking is about passing judgement on other people, based on the information that you have on hand. Critical thinking is far from this, in fact, it is considerably deeper in its intent. Critical thinking is all about decision making, and helping a person get to the best possible decision following information analysis that is based on a range of perspectives.

In the chapters of this book, you have learned all about what critical thinking actually is and how you can use it in your life. In addition, you also know about the stages of critical thinking and the skills that are necessary to master critical thinking and make it a permanent part of your life. Critical thinking can be applied to every area of your life, in a professional as well as social manner. This is because you make hundreds of problem solving decisions each day, and having critical thinking at your fingertips will ensure that the decisions you make are well thought out and offer viable solutions to all problems.

With critical thinking, you stop yourself from thinking harder in order to arrive at a solution. Instead, you enjoy the benefits of thinking better, no matter what challenge that you find yourself up against.